LEAD!

RICHARD LYNCH

LEAD!

HOW PUBLIC AND NONPROFIT MANAGERS CAN BRING OUT THE BEST IN THEMSELVES AND THEIR ORGANIZATIONS

Jossey-Bass Publishers · San Francisco

For sales outside the United States, contact Maxwell Macmillan International Publishing Group, 866 Third Avenue, New York, New York 10022.

Manufactured in the United States of America

 The paper used in this book is acid-free and meets the State of California requirements for recycled paper (50 percent recycled waste, including 10 percent postconsumer waste), which are the strictest guidelines for recycled paper currently in use in the United States.

Library of Congress Cataloging-in-Publication Data

Lynch, Richard, date.
    Lead! : how public and nonprofit managers can bring out the best in themselves and their organizations / Richard Lynch. — 1st ed.
       p.   cm.—(The Jossey-Bass nonprofit sector series) (The Jossey-Bass public administration series)
    Includes bibliographical references and index.
    ISBN 1-55542-494-5
    1. Leadership. 2. Executive ability. 3. Organizational change.
I. Title. II. Series. III. Series: The Jossey-Bass public administration series.
HD57.7.L96   1993
658.4'09—dc20   92-1708
                                              CIP

FIRST EDITION
HB Printing   10 9 8 7 6 5 4 3 2 1   *Code 9295*

A joint publication in

The Jossey-Bass
Nonprofit Sector Series
and
The Jossey-Bass
Public Administration Series

CONTENTS

PREFACE

In today's government and nonprofit organizations, there is a new cry for leadership. Old ways of doing things are no longer good enough for the clients of those organizations or for the people who serve them. People are growing frustrated with services that require large sums of money but have little impact, and with management procedures that waste people's lives in bureaucratic routine. *LEAD!* speaks to those who hold management positions in such organizations and who want to play a leadership role in developing them to their full potential. It is a book for managers who want to bring out the best in their people.

My mother, age seventy-six, worked for most of her professional life at the Illinois State Geological Survey. Last year, she ran into the person who, twenty years later, holds her old job. "You're Betty Lynch?" the woman exclaimed. "You're legendary!" It isn't often that one hears a state employee described in such terms. What the woman meant, of course, is that my mother made a memorable contribution to her institution, a contribution that is remembered and admired by people twenty years later. This is a book about encouraging that sort of performance by all the people who work for an organization.

Background and Audience

What people are capable of doing is the greatest unexploited resource of any organization. *LEAD!* is a book for managers who want to tap that potential. By following the advice offered here, managers in government and nonprofit organizations can create a work situation that builds their people's competence and self-esteem and makes possible legendary performance.

The book presents a theory of leadership based on my seventeen years of consulting with managers in all walks of life. It tells you how to develop your own and your organization's power; how to get the job done effectively, deliver service that makes a difference, and promote worker satisfaction. Leaders do these things by encouraging performance that is above expectations and above the norm. This book describes how to bring out the best in people through effective leadership.

Where there is effective leadership, people's lives take on a sense of meaning that they traditionally find only away from work, if at all. Where there is leadership, the work experience enhances people's self-esteem. Where there is leadership, community problems are solved, clients' lives are made better, and citizens' needs are met. Gradually, such a situation is evolving. Slowly, government organizations are finding new ways of doing things and (more quickly) nonprofit organizations are finding new approaches to prospering. Progress is uneven, however, as one organization takes a step forward and another is mired in bureaucratic complacency.

People who take leadership positions in such organizations often have no role models to guide them in how to proceed. Books, tapes, and lectures on leadership are almost exclusively directed toward the private sector. The unique problems of the public and nonprofit sectors are frequently overlooked. Books that do address those sectors are designed to impart a theoretical understanding of leadership; they are often short on practical advice. The reader is left to translate the material for practical application. *LEAD!* tells people who aspire to be leaders how to fulfill an often unfamiliar but essential role.

The book is unique not only in its practical focus but also in its application of psychological theory to the role of the leader. The material concerning the effect leaders have on people's willingness to work is based on the psychological research of William Glasser, Martin Seligman, Harris Clemes, and Reynold Bean, among others. The application of this material to leadership can help us understand why some leaders have such a dramatic effect on other people's behavior.

A third way in which this book differs from others on leadership is that it is not aimed solely at top managers. I believe that, for an organization to prosper, managers at all levels must behave like leaders. Top leaders in large organizations need to foster leadership in their middle-level managers and frontline supervisors, or the effects of their own leadership will become muted or lost in the intervening layers of management.

The material presented here is based largely on my experience as a consultant and trainer. In leading approximately 150 seminars a year for government and nonprofit managers, I have an opportunity to hear of their triumphs and tribulations firsthand. I also have a chance to survey managers on many of the topics covered in this book, such as team building. Much of the information here is anecdotal and based on what has worked for people in leadership situations. The book's theory builds on other books about leadership, such as Kouzes and Posner's *The Leadership Challenge* (1989), Senge's *The Fifth Discipline* (1990), and Zaleznik's *The Managerial Mystique* (1989).

The skills and tasks discussed in the chapters of this book equip leaders to create the conditions necessary for legendary performance. These are not the nuts-and-bolts managerial skills of planning, budgeting, coaching, delegating, and measuring performance. Although such skills are certainly necessary for leaders, exercising them is management, not leadership. To lead, people must first have managed to the point where they are able to turn their attention away from the deluge of daily demands and lift their eyes to the horizon.

Overview of the Contents

The first of the three parts of this book is concerned with self-development and describes who leaders are, the importance of their role, and how they acquire the ability to influence others. To lead, one must have followers. People in leadership positions must have power or influence over the people they supervise. In this first part, we explore the roots of such influence and what potential leaders can do to enhance their power. Chapter One introduces the concept of leadership and tells how it is different from traditional management. Chapter Two explains how to tap the potential influence inherent in a leader's status or position in the hierarchy. Chapter Three describes how to enhance one's influence by developing one's own personal power.

Leaders are agents of movement, agents of change. To be effective, however, change must be purposeful. The second part of the book deals with the creation of a purpose and a system for moving toward it. It is devoted to the leader's role in providing a sense of direction and a vehicle for reaching the goal. The emphasis is on the leader's role in developing systems and structures that bring out the best in people. Chapter Four explains how leaders, with the help of their followers, create a sense of purpose by defining a mission and sense of vision for the organization. Chapter Five describes how leaders create a system that produces effective and purposeful movement toward the mission. Chapter Six discusses how leaders design jobs that motivate employees by connecting them to meaningful results. Chapter Seven summarizes how managers can create a streamlined system by using the principles explained in Chapters Four, Five, and Six.

The third and final part of this book discusses the relationship between leaders and their people. I believe that effective leadership works because the process of moving toward the organization's purpose builds people's self-esteem. Chapter Eight explains how leaders enunciate and enforce values, and Chapter Nine describes how leaders keep their people hopeful in the face of adversity. Chapter Ten discusses methods of creating a positive organizational climate. In a sense, this last chapter explores the consequences of all the material presented earlier. It explores the effects of leaders' actions on the organizational climate and explains how those effects influence the self-esteem of the people being led.

Seattle, Washington   Richard Lynch
September 1992

THE AUTHOR

Richard Lynch is a Seattle-based management consultant with a variety of clients across North America. He works primarily with nonprofit organizations and local government on ways to achieve greater results with less cost and effort, through streamlining organizational structures, setting performance standards, developing evaluation systems, identifying obstacles to productivity, and assessing the motivational "health" of organizations. Lynch also speaks to approximately five thousand people a year at workshops, conventions, and conferences in North America and Britain on topics related to personal growth and management effectiveness.

He is the author of the books *Precision Management* (1988) and *Getting Out of Your Own Way* (1989) and of a monograph entitled "Developing Your Leadership Potential" (1988). He is coauthor of the books *Essential Volunteer Management* (1989, with S. McCurley) and *Secrets of Leadership* (1991, with S. Vineyard) and is a regular contributor to professional journals.

Lynch received his B.A. degree (1966) in history from the University of Illinois and his M.A. degree (1968) in the history of ideas from the University of Iowa. Before starting his own firm in 1977, he worked for two New York-based consulting firms. He has worked as a volunteer coordinator and as training director for the Washington State Office of Voluntary Action, where he set up a unique system of delivering management training to volunteer directors through a network of volunteer training organizers. He has also served on the boards of directors of several nonprofit organizations, including a volunteer center, a retired senior volunteer program, the United Way, and national and local literacy programs.

LEAD!

PART ONE

BRING OUT THE BEST IN YOURSELF

Chapter One

Your Role as a Leader

Quietly, a revolution in leadership is occurring across North America, a revolution that is unlocking the full performance potential of the people who work in our businesses, government, and nonprofit organizations. Spurred by competitive pressures, leaders in business are setting the pace, but signs of the revolution are also appearing in other sectors of our society. This book is intended for managers of government or nonprofit organizations who seek to join this revolution and tap the full potential of their organizations to make a difference in the world.

As the pace of change accelerates, the need for leadership becomes more critical. Those who continue to manage in the old ways will find their organizations in crisis. The credibility of such organizations to actually do something about the problems they are supposed to solve is dropping among taxpayers and donors in many communities. Managers who for years have equated the amount of money they spend with how much they are doing about a problem are now encountering skepticism. Joseph Sensenbrenner, former mayor of Madison, Wisconsin, put it this way: "People don't believe

3

that government knows how to help or wants to bother" (Sensenbrenner, 1991, p. 64). Consequently, budgets come under pressure,
and the number of people in need grows.

In 1990, David Osborne described the current situation in his
advice to the new mayor of Washington, D.C. "The kind of governments that developed during the 1930s, 1940s, and 1950s, with their
sluggish centralized bureaucracies, their preoccupation with rules
and regulations, and their hierarchical chains of command, no
longer work very well. . . . The environment changed, and they
failed to change with it. Hierarchical centralized bureaucracies
simply do not function well in the rapidly changing, information-
rich, knowledge-intensive society and economy of the 1990s" (Osborne, p. 20).

Such a situation cries out for more than merely managing
things as they are. If we are to be a workable society, if we are to
make the world a better place in which to live, those in management
positions must lead as well as manage. In towns and cities, counties,
and states, in voluntary groups and nonprofit organizations, people
are beginning to respond to this challenge. Managers at all levels
of government and nonprofit organizations are beginning to revitalize their institutions, to free our organizations from bureaucratic
entanglements and the politics of self-interest, to breath new life
into our efforts to solve our social problems and provide for the
common good. In short, they are beginning to lead.

Leaders and Leadership

In this book, the term *leadership* does not apply only to those at the
top of organizational pyramids. Vital organizations have leaders at all
levels of management. To respond quickly to changing circumstances, first-line and middle-level managers must exercise leadership.

Although employers and boards of directors often speak of
seeking people with "leadership potential," they are often unable
to define what leadership is. They assume that leaders are individuals with certain inborn, amorphous traits that allow them to mag-
ically galvanize others. Many studies of leadership and a growing
body of anecdotal evidence have shown that leadership involves a
group of skills and productive habits of behavior and thought.

While the skills and habits of leadership are more difficult to learn than those of, say, driving a car, they can nonetheless be acquired by people who want to develop their leadership potential. This book is a guide to those who wish to play a leadership role in their organizations.

At the outset, however, I should caution the reader that peril lurks in playing such a role. Many organizations today do not provide a very hospitable climate for leadership. As Abraham Zaleznik (1989) points out in *The Managerial Mystique,* many organizations today suffer from a lack of leadership but operate in such a way that the remedy is very difficult. One who begins to assume a leadership role is often seen as a disruptive influence and a threat to the established order. Tom Peters, in his speeches on this subject, sometimes asks his audience, "If you were running an automotive company, would you hire Soichiro Honda?" Given the fact that Honda rose from humble beginnings to create and lead one of the most successful companies in the world, most people would say yes. Peters then goes on to focus on Honda's quirky and irascible personality, noting that in most modern organizations he would be fired, passed over, or isolated as a maverick.

This is not to say that all leaders are difficult to get along with. But the very nature of leadership often causes leaders to act in ways that senior managers or boards of directors with greater authority in the organization usually resist. These people tend to have a vested interest in the status quo, and leaders are people who foment change. Soichiro Honda had a passion for change, a passion for improvement that made his company the source of many breakthroughs in automotive and engine technology. Such a person's superiors often feel uncomfortable about this passion, particularly if they identify strongly with existing procedures. As a result, the very behavior that will revitalize our organizations is seen as a threat by those who manage them.

Twenty years ago, when I worked for a community action agency in Alabama, I came across a typewritten paper by a community organizer named Nicholas Von Hoffman, who at that time worked for the Industrial Areas Foundation in Chicago. In it, he offered a definition of how to identify a community leader that cuts through a great deal of the mystery that surrounds leadership in today's literature: a leader is a person who has a following. Although this statement may seem self-evident, it contains many important implications that enable us to analyze more clearly what leadership is and what it takes to develop leadership potential. Again, a leader is any person who has a following. Leadership, then, is the ability to influence others to follow.

People tend to think of leaders as people who influence others to follow by the power of their charismatic personality. We think, for example, of Martin Luther King's stirring speeches or of Winston Churchill's galvanizing pronouncements. Followers gain self-confidence when they hear such leaders speak. The charismatic leader articulates the needs and aspirations of the followers and imparts to them feelings of power and effectiveness. He or she gives them hope and builds their self-esteem. However, leaders can produce these effects regardless of whether they have a personality that is traditionally labeled charismatic.

In addition to having a following, a leader must move. You cannot be a leader if you are standing still, if you are content with things as they are. You can manage things as they are, but you are not leading if you are content to do tomorrow what you did yesterday.

This means that the greatest enemy of leaders is the status quo. Leaders are relentless enemies of the daily routine and the standard operating procedure. They burn with a desire to make the present system obsolete, to create a better future. Where there is no leadership, organizations often wind up defending the status quo long after the quo has lost its status.

In the face of adversity, this future focus is particularly critical. When things go wrong, leaders ask, "How can we do better next time?" or "What can this experience teach us that will make us stronger in the future?" Such questions build hope by focusing people's attention on the future and the group rather than on recriminations about an individual's performance in the past. But such a future focus is also important when things are going well. Leaders, in Zaleznik's words, realize that "past formulas for success today contain the seeds of decay" (1992, p. 130). In their passion for improvement, they keep their organizations from stagnating in a changing world.

Leaders Versus Traditional Managers

Leaders and traditional managers have different views of change. Instead of looking on change as a necessary reaction to outside forces, leaders initiate change. While traditional managers, wedded to the status quo, frequently see change as a threat, leaders look forward to change as an opportunity to grow, to gain advantage, and to prosper. They thus inspire creativity in their paid and volunteer staffs. They focus their group on making something new, exciting, and effective.

Leaders see the future as something to create, while traditional managers see it as something to react to. Traditional managers look at change as something that causes problems, and they spend their days in furious problem-solving behavior. Their point of view is "How can we continue to make our present systems work in the face of new realities?" Leaders, on the other hand, are not concerned with maintaining the security of business as usual. They see the future as filled with opportunities to create something better than the present system. Leaders have a passion for positive innovation. If a person is not trying to improve things, she or he is not leading.

These and other differences between successful leaders and traditional managers are summarized in the following list.

1. Managers make sure that things work well. Leaders create that which works better.
2. Managers solve today's problems by smoothing out the difficulties brought on by changing events. Leaders create a better future by seizing opportunities stimulated by changing events.
3. Managers focus on the process. Leaders focus on the product.
4. Managers make sure the details are taken care of. Leaders set broad purposes and directions.
5. Managers make sure that people put in an honest day's work for an honest day's pay. Leaders inspire people to do more than expected.
6. Managers organize and plan to meet this year's objectives. Leaders create a vision of the organization several years hence.
7. Managers create efficient policies and standard operating

procedures. Leaders go beyond the need for standard procedures and create a more effective system.

8. Managers focus on efficiency. Leaders focus on effectiveness.
9. Managers focus on problem behavior and seek to improve it
   through counseling, coaching, and nurturing. Leaders focus
   on what is going right and praise it.
10. Managers worry about the present. Leaders look forward to
    the future.

Leading and Managing

Both leading and managing are crucial to the success of a modern
organization. Those in leadership positions must, of necessity,
manage as well as lead. In fact, one must manage effectively in order
to be able to lead. When things are poorly managed, turmoil and
alienation of the work force result. Managers become so immersed
in worrying about the details of other people's jobs that they have
no time for thinking positively about the future. They and their
subordinates are under a great deal of stress just dealing with the
present. When people are under stress, they do not take risks and
therefore do not grow. When an organization is under stress, it is
more focused on survival than on moving confidently into the future. Leadership is possible, therefore, only when one has managed
to the point that things are going reasonably well and people can
lift their heads from the frustration of their daily routine and start
to think about how they can make a difference.

In addition, leaders need managers to handle the details of
making the vision come to pass. However, those managers also
should assume a leadership role with the people they manage. To
be effective, an organization needs both leaders and managers.

I once consulted with a fire department that had a morale
problem. One of the major irritants was the fact that the chief was
immersed in the details of everything that went on in the department. He scheduled drills, ordered uniforms, decided what businesses should be inspected, ordered supplies, and even got down
under the fire engines when they were in the shop for maintenance
to tell the mechanic what to do. I recommended that he delegate
authority for these things to his two assistant chiefs, four captains,

and the fire fighters themselves. His response was, "Then what would *I* do?"

My answer was, lead. Focus on creating a vision of a better future. Create a positive, esteem-building organizational climate. Create a system that builds commitment. Build effective teams. Help people feel important. Establish values. Generate a passion for the purpose of the organization. All of this is "soft stuff." It is not the nuts and bolts of doing the work, but most people rise to leadership positions because of their expertise in managing and even doing the work. It is hardly surprising, then, that so little effective leadership is displayed in our organizations today. Leadership tasks require new skills that people have never had to use before.

Being effective in leadership also requires a love for engaging in the foregoing kinds of tasks. Effective leaders realize that by doing so they create more satisfying lives for the people who work for them and for the people the organization serves. There is no more noble purpose than this.

Making Things Happen

Successful leaders have many traits in common, but above all, leaders are people who make things happen. As opposed to the vast majority who muddle along, successful leaders do not merely react to the demands of outside forces. They do not wait for others to goad them to action. Rather than merely responding to circumstances, they act with a purpose. In other words, successful leaders are proactive instead of reactive. Rather than spending life mired in the demands of others, leaders cause things to happen. They have an effect on events and gain a sense of being in control of their own lives.

The vast majority of people in our society are reactive. By not developing the quality of proactive thinking, they eliminate their leadership potential. Reactive people work only on what someone else requires them to work on. Anything that is not urgent is put off until it is urgent, a habit that leads to paralyzing procrastination. Worse, things that will never be urgent are never pursued.

The toll this takes on one's capacity for success is illustrated by an acquaintance of mine who operates a small business in Seattle. For eight years, whenever I have seen him, he has talked to me about an idea he has for his business that will transform it from its present small size into a highly successful and profitable venture that will make life much better for him and for his customers. A careful search through his files reveals one very thin folder that relates to this project. In this folder are some lists of things he intends to do someday. This is as far as he has gotten in eight years.

The reason that he has made no more progress than this has nothing to do with the idea itself. It is probably a very good idea. It would not take much capital to put it into practice. It would not even be very hard to do. The only thing wrong with the idea is that it has no deadline. It will never be urgent. No one will be upset with the business owner if he never follows through on it. The problem is that he is, as most of us are, a reactive person, a person who does not take action on something unless it is urgent. Every day he goes to work and finds something urgent that demands his attention. The idea will always take a backseat to other things until everything that has a deadline is completed, which is to say never.

The habit of putting off ideas until "someday" leaves people wishing at the end of life that they had taken the time to turn their ideas into reality. Or it leads them to rage in jealous disappointment when someone else does what they had for years only dreamed of doing. Such situations cry out for leadership, for someone to cause the change without being pressed to do so. This requires commitment to making a difference. When one leads, one begins to unleash the enthusiasm of others for fulfilling the idea or the purpose of the organization.

Sometimes people take no action because they feel powerless to do anything. Laws, regulations, or policies mandate the status quo. But human beings make these rules and human beings can change them. For example, Laura Lee Geraghty, director of the Minnesota Office on Volunteer Services, saw a need for liability protection for volunteers serving in nonprofit organizations. Mobilizing the efforts of volunteers across the state in 1987, she succeeded in getting legislation passed to provide such coverage. The following year, she completed a similar campaign to cover volunteers in government. She and the volunteers expended all this energy because they were committed to meeting the need. Leaders, filled with a commitment to the purpose of the organization, hack away at the weeds of regulation that threaten to obscure or strangle their vision.

Building Leadership Success

To be effective as leaders we must focus our people's energies on the purpose of the organization. We must get them to work on things according to their importance, according to the difference they will make. Only in this way can we and they build success. To succeed, we must deliberately choose to make things happen.

Let me give an example of how a leader works in this way. One of the most successful school principals in the United States works in an elementary school in the Cincinnati area. Though neither rich nor famous, she would have to be regarded as highly successful, given the academic achievement and good behavior of her students. Here are a few of the proactive steps she has taken to make her school so outstanding:

> Starting a "Bring Up Your Grades" club (the BUG club), with special privileges for students who bring their grades up a whole grade level
>
> Getting parents to win prizes at Kings Island amusement park and donate them to the school to be used as awards
>
> Establishing a student-of-the-month award for a student in each class, who is honored, given an award, and has his or her picture displayed on a hall bulletin board
>
> Having every school employee "adopt" a low-achieving student with the goal of getting the student into the BUG club
>
> Getting a local cookie store to donate a cookie to each student who makes any outstanding achievement in the school
>
> Giving awards for good school citizenship, such as picking up trash on the playground
>
> Recruiting volunteers to bind stories written by students into books that can be checked out of the library

These and many other small ideas have focused the students' attention on positive behavior and created a climate conducive to learning. They are all examples of the proactive behavior of a person making things happen rather than waiting for things to happen to her. We could contrast her behavior with that of the typical principal, who is too busy with administrative meetings, the lunch count, disciplinary actions, and teacher complaints to make anything meaningful happen. We could contrast her with principals who have been ground down by the system, who may once have had dreams but who never got around to fulfilling them and now dismiss them as unrealistic. We could contrast her with principals who greet every new idea with a variety of excuses for why it cannot be implemented. For example, as I was describing this principal in one of my leadership seminars, I heard a principal in the audience say to a colleague, "I couldn't do that. I don't have a cookie store near my school."

Such an attitude condemns that principal to the mediocrity of the status quo. He will live out his professional life in the anxiety of meeting deadlines and requirements. Actions such as those listed above will never be "due first" because the Cincinnati principal took none of them in response to district requirements.

One of the most common excuses reactive people use is that they have so many requirements to meet they have no time for anything "extra." By taking the time to make the positive changes in her school, however, the principal in Cincinnati greatly reduced the amount of time she had to spend on disciplinary actions and counseling of teachers who were having a hard time getting their students to concentrate on learning. By taking the time to be proactive in this way, leaders find they have less to react to.

Distinguishing Four Types of Activity

Leaders must prioritize their work according to proactive criteria. They must set proactive goals and give first priority to making progress toward them so as to escape a life of merely reacting to the urgent. As Alec MacKenzie (1975) points out in *The Time Trap*, most people regard any task that is urgent as being important, but the two things are not necessarily the same. Any task we might engage in can be classified as being urgent or not urgent and as having high payoff or low payoff. Urgent means that the task absolutely has to be done now: someone wants us to finish it soon. High payoff means that completing the task will have some positive consequence or benefit for the people served or for the organization itself. Stephen Covey (1990) defines four general classes of activity on which we can spend our time. To paraphrase him, the four types are as follows:

1. Tasks that are both urgent and have high payoff
2. Tasks that are not urgent but have high payoff
3. Tasks that are urgent but have low payoff
4. Tasks that are not urgent and have low payoff

An example of the first type of task would be that of a volunteer director in city government finishing a proposal to his boss that will result in a city policy promoting the use of volunteers in all departments. Because the boss must have the proposal by 3:00 tomorrow afternoon so that she can take it to the city council meeting, the task is urgent. If adopted, the proposal will lend additional status to volunteers in the city and make the volunteer program stronger, so the task has a high payoff.

The second type of activity is the most critical for leaders to pay attention to—the tasks that make a positive difference but are not urgent. By not urgent, I mean there is plenty of time to get them done. There will be no negative consequence (except that an opportunity will be lost) if they are not done now. These include actions such as those taken by the principal mentioned earlier. If she had never taken any of those actions, no one would have been upset; things would have gone on as before.

Type three activities are urgent but have low impact. For example, one of the engineers in a state highway department was asked by his boss to respond to a professional magazine survey by calculating how many tons of concrete had been laid in the state the previous year according to type of concrete and use. The magazine needed the information by the end of the week. All fifty states had been asked to respond to the survey. If the engineer had not completed the survey, the magazine would have noted that his state had not responded. By taking the time to research and calculate the requested information, he was not furthering his success in his field and career or helping his organization fulfill its mission. Nonetheless, the task was urgent. There was a deadline.

Modern organizations waste vast amounts of time on these third-class pursuits. One museum, for example, recently moved its sixty staff people to a new location. To accomplish this, it created an "office move team" of employees to handle the logistics of the move. The team coordinator decided to establish eight subcommittees within the team:

1. A subcommittee to write a request for proposals from moving companies
2. A time line subcommittee to develop a plan for the move
3. A subcommittee to create a relocation manual to tell the staff all the things they had to do to prepare for the move
4. A subcommittee to create a facilities orientation manual to familiarize the staff with the new offices
5. A subcommittee to determine what furniture, fixtures, and equipment would be moved to the new location
6. A subcommittee to determine what files and records to keep, to move, and to discard
7. A subcommittee to assess the need for and to recruit volunteers to help with the move
8. A communications subcommittee to develop signs, maps, and directories to guide the moving company during the move

Suppose that one Wednesday afternoon, you were working on your section of the relocation manual. If you did not finish it by three o'clock, it would not be printed in time to be distributed to all employees. So the task would be urgent. In reality, however, the relocation manual itself would have a low payoff in terms of the organization's purpose. It would not even have much impact on the efficiency of the move. Most people probably would not even read it. Meanwhile, you would be taking time away from high-payoff pursuits.

Leaders in the 1990s must show no tolerance for such activities. They must free their people from activities that blunt their efforts and make legendary performance impossible. They must focus people on the organization's purpose and take the most direct route to an outcome. Contrast the museum manager who instituted the office move team with a leader in a government office of similar size. The day before the move, he told the members of his staff to put all their belongings in boxes on top of their desks and to report for work early at the new offices to help guide the movers the next day. This procedure may have been less structured than the museum's, but it got the job done with a much smaller expenditure of valuable staff time.

Activities of the fourth type are neither urgent nor of high payoff. Although these involve proactive tasks, they have little impact on the organization or on the people that it serves. For example, I once encountered a manager poring over a book of sample typefaces in order to find a new one in which to print the report of his monthly staff meeting. By selecting a more pleasing typeface, he was doing something that had little impact on his organization or on his career. The activity was also not urgent in that no one would care if it were left undone. Although most people don't think they spend much time on activities of this type, most people turn to them when the pressure is off.

The vast majority of people begin each workday with the question "What is the most urgent thing I have to do today?" They direct their attention first to what is due first, second to what is due second, and so on. This habit produces the stress of constantly responding to other people's demands. It is the habit of a person who will tend to muddle through life but never make anything happen.

In the stress of responding to the demands of outside forces, people tend to lose sight of their purpose. The distinction between what will make a difference and what will not begins to blur. Eventually, the only distinction between one activity and another is the due date. It's all just "stuff to do." Their primary motivation at work becomes fear, fear that someone else will be upset if they do not get a thing done by a certain time. It is impossible to be effective and successful in this situation.

Such reactive work habits not only limit a person's ability to be an effective leader but also to be an effective follower. Followers' abilities and creativity are snuffed out in the drudgery of responding to deadlines. Minimum rather than legendary performance is the result.

In order to be effective, a leader must be able to lift her gaze from the dusty road of the standard operating procedure and keep her eyes on the horizon. She must have the courage to set as priorities those tasks and projects that will create a better future. This requires a great deal of personal power, self-confidence, and resolve, saying no to the trivial demands of others and yes to the tasks that are required only by her vision.

Developing Proactive Thinking and Behavior

Leaders help others become more proactive by getting them to focus on the purpose of the enterprise and by encouraging creative ideas. Without such a sense of purpose and empowerment, proactive thinking and behavior are unlikely. If people believe that work is only a series of required activities, they will never contribute anything extra. If they are passionate about the purpose of the work, however, and if they believe the leader will value their ideas, they will find ways to make something happen. Thus, leaders replace the motivation of fear with the motivation of achievement. They enrich the work lives of their people while making the organization stronger.

An effective leader works with others to develop a vision of where the organization is going, a vision of a better future for the organization. The people being led can then internalize a detailed picture of what kind of future they are trying to create. This produces a common purpose and a sense of excitement. Part of this vision is the sense of change that will be wrought in the world through the accomplishment of the organization's strategic goals. The other part is more internal. It is a vivid sense of what the organization will look like, what it will do, and how it will be regarded in the future.

The vision is best created with the involvement of the followers. The leader can facilitate this involvement by having small groups of people answer this question: "If we were going to go across the street and start a competing organization, what would we do over there to make our present organization obsolete?" The question helps people escape the bonds of what is, so that they can think about what ought to be. It therefore helps the organization escape the trap of its own procedures so that it can renew itself. In a competitive environment, this question keeps the group ahead of the competition. If the group itself does not ask this question today, someone else will ask it tomorrow.

In responding to this question, people need plenty of time to work on their ideas about the future. The exercise should be carefully prepared and thoughtfully completed. In conducting such an exercise with a state employment service agency, I gave each of the groups a formal request for proposal (RFP) and asked them to prepare a formal presentation. Although I had given them the entire afternoon to do this, some groups were still working at midnight.

An illustration of the process comes from a community organization. The mission of the group was to meet the recreational needs of the community. It raised money through bingo and other special events and received technical assistance from the city parks department. The organization had built a hall and a skating rink in a local park and equipped hockey, soccer, and softball teams that each played in a city league. Volunteers, board members, and staff discussed what they would do if they were to start a competing organization across the street. I asked them to create an organization that would be more appealing than their present one to both citizens and volunteers. Following is a list of some of their ideas.

Offer twenty-four-hour child care
Have a party room with a hot tub and Jacuzzi
Offer aerobics classes
Provide large and small rooms for community activities
Own a bus that would take residents to the hall
Give fashion shows
Install an island kitchen with microwave ovens
Have a well-trained executive board skilled in volunteer
    management
Own a welcome wagon
Encourage a neighborhood pub to open next door
Sponsor neighborhood picnics and block parties
Begin an adopt-a-neighbor program
Install plush carpeting
Provide a pool table and a Ping-Pong table

Own a carpentry shop that could be rented out to community
    residents
Conduct board meetings in luxurious locations
Provide good toys for children
Put in a good sound system
Hold dances
Install skateboard ramps
Operate a sports equipment store at the hall

After groups come up with a list such as this, the tendency
is to say, "But we could never do that. It would take too much
money. It isn't realistic." The truth of the matter is, however, that
with enough desire, people can create anything they can imagine.
And if they refuse to imagine a better situation, they are unlikely
to get one. It is such circumstances that test the quality of the leader.
If the leader allows herself and her group to be stopped by the
thought that the idea is something that they can never do, she has
abandoned her primary role as a maker of change. If the leader can
be stopped by a thought in her head, what will she do when she
encounters a real obstacle?

I firmly believe that there are people who are illiterate, angry,
hungry, destructive, or isolated in our society today because in the
agencies that are available to serve them, a leader allowed the
thought "we can't do that" to kill a good idea. I believe there are
businesses that are struggling because their leaders refuse to commit
their organizations to the task of creating the possible. To be effective, leaders have to make things happen. They do this by encouraging people to imagine a better situation and then committing
the necessary resources to help that come about.

Several of the community organization's ideas did indeed
cost a great deal more money than the organization had on hand.
At the same time, however, several of them were also income-
generating ideas. The role of the leader is to help the group discard
any ideas that seem unwise to pursue and then to bring together the
remaining ideas, the ideas the group can really get excited about,
into a coherent vision of what the organization intends to become.

Here are some ideas generated in a similar exercise by local leaders of a national organization whose purpose is to fight a debilitating and deadly disease:

> Recruit a media personality to serve as a spokesperson for us
> Develop a strong affiliation with a health care institution
> Provide in-home visits to patients suffering from the disease
> Conduct a "splashy" public education campaign so people will know what we do and why we do it
> Rent a storefront office for greater visibility
> Obtain an 800 number
> Have a drive-up window where people can pick up information about the disease

> Some other examples of the fruits of the RFP process follow.

County Government

Eliminate line-item budgets for each department
Hold each department head responsible for the achievement of goals rather than the spending of money
Eliminate the personnel department and give each department full authority to hire the best people
Enable managers who underspend their budgets to be rewarded by carrying the funds over to the next year instead of punished by being given a smaller budget
Set up an alternative career track so that people can receive an increase in salary without necessarily going into management

Battered women's shelter

Develop a business in the community to support the shelter
Provide a larger facility with private rooms for each family
Prepare an alumni directory
Do follow-up on former clients
Provide counseling rooms

State cooperative extension program

Publish a "Dr. Information" column in the local newspaper
Develop a uniform symbol (akin to McDonald's golden arches) to make it easy to find extension service offices

Develop a computer-based filing system to get quick access
to information clients need

Advertise "one-hour service" in response to questions from
the public

Provide child-care services to volunteers and staff

Develop intergenerational programs for families

Hospital maternity unit

Offer private rooms

Provide double beds so that husbands can stay

Use satin sheets

Add a courtyard outside the rooms

Provide designer uniforms for nurses

Library

Design window displays of new books

Order enough popular books so that people don't have to
wait for them

Provide study rooms

Provide a reading lounge and make coffee and ice cream
available

Offer twenty-four-hour research service

Provide computers with popular software

Offer students homework assistance

Have a courtyard for reading

As shown in these examples, the kinds of ideas that tend to
dominate such lists are ideas for the improvement of the internal
operations of the organization. These provide a nice complement to
strategic goals, which are externally focused. The combination of
the two creates a vibrant picture of what the organization intends
to become, a purpose that gives meaning to the day-to-day duties
of each group member.

None of these ideas had been considered by any of the participants before they were given the challenge to think proactively.
Each idea represents a proactive task, a task that will make a difference for the organization and the people it serves. Carrying out
any of them helps make the organization and the individual leader

more successful. It enables the leader to be known as the person who developed the public education (or some other) campaign instead of the person who struggles into the night to meet the requirements of others.

Creating a Phantom Competitor

The exercise of starting a competing organization across the street can be especially helpful in leading an organization that has a monopoly on the business of its clients. When people work in a monopoly, they tend to serve the system rather than the customer. They are judged and rewarded on the basis of their impact on the ease of doing things or on their enhancement of the organization's standing. Or they are judged by how much money they have spent, whether that money was used to do something about a problem or expand the bureaucracy. They become immersed in their procedures, internal processes, and career mobility, and the mission of the organization gets obscured.

One publicly financed transportation system, for example, sold commuter tickets to those who used the service frequently. This meant that regular commuters didn't have to wait in line with other passengers for tickets. In the early eighties, however, the organization put in computerized cash registers. They were hooked up to a mainframe computer at headquarters that counted the number of people buying tickets each day. This information did not give an accurate account of the number of people using the service each day, however, because the majority used commuter tickets. To increase the quality of its information system, management began to require the commuters to stand in line with the other passengers and hand their ticket to a clerk who would enter the information in the computer. This pleased management by improving the quality of the information, but it greatly irritated people whose commuting time was increased by a half-hour wait in line each day.

One of the reasons why people lose sight of the purpose of such a monopolistic organization is that the customers have no ability to take their business elsewhere, and the organization can come to regard its customers as a bother rather than as a reason for its existence. When the customer is regarded as a nuisance, the likelihood of legendary service is remote. I recently traveled by Amtrak from Chicago to Champaign, Illinois. At the start of our journey, the conductor announced over a loudspeaker, "On our trip you must not change seats. Anyone who changes seats will be removed from this train. Also, your carry-on luggage must go in the overhead racks. Anyone who puts luggage in a seat will be removed from this train." Threatening the customer in this way is something that seldom happens on an airplane because the customer generally has a choice of carriers.

Years ago, when Peter Johnson (1988) was the head of Bonneville Power, a public agency that supplies electricity to northwestern utilities, he grappled with the problems of operating a monopoly business. He came up with the concept of the phantom competitor, an imaginary, competing power supplier. When problems arose, he would ask his people, "What is the phantom competitor doing about this problem?" This question tended to unleash creativity and produce the kind of response that would have occurred if there had indeed been an agency competitor.

Creating such an imaginary foe can help keep your organization sharp. In times of funding difficulty, for example, you might tell your people to imagine that there is a competing organization across the street and ask them what the competitor is doing to solve its funding crisis. In good times, the phantom competitor can also be used to ward off complacency. "What are they doing across the street to try to get our clients to go over there? What are they doing to convince our funding sources that their money will be better spent over there? How are they managing their key people so that they keep them committed and motivated?" These and similar questions can stimulate employees' creative thinking and help keep them focused on the needs of the people they serve.

In addition to stimulating the creative imagination of their people, leaders can also get good ideas from similar organizations in other communities. Although there may only be one crisis clinic in a given town, for example, there are other clinics in other cities that may have developed in creative new directions. By talking frequently to peers, a leader can bring successful new approaches to the attention of the group.

Taking Action

Success requires much more than gathering ideas and setting a goal, of course. It requires perseverance and the ability to devote time to achieving that goal. Some say that it is the dreamers who make a difference. But in my experience it is not a lack of dreaming but a lack of taking action to turn those dreams into reality that causes most people to be less than successful. Martin Luther King, for example, not only had a dream, but made things happen, things that brought his dream closer to reality.

As already noted, proactive people find the time to make things happen. If you carve out the time to implement ideas such as those listed earlier, you will find that by causing things to happen, you will reduce the number of things to which you must react. You will recall that by implementing her proactive ideas, the Cincinnati school principal found she did not have to spend nearly as much time responding to disciplinary problems. This same reduction in "reaction time" occurred in most of the individual cases mentioned in this chapter. Proactive people are quick to discover this reduction, leaving their reactive counterparts wondering how they ever find the time to accomplish so many important tasks.

Another way in which proactive people get the time to pursue their ideas relates to the fact that the time it takes to accomplish any given task is very elastic. Many people who feel they could never find the time to pursue a proactive idea, nonetheless manage to take time off to be sick for a day or two or to go on vacation or to attend a seminar. They could, in fact, also take that day or two to devote their energies to making something happen. This is one of the secrets of successful people. If you take the time to be proactive, you will find that the things you have been reacting to will shrink, just as they do when you are not there at all.

Still another way in which leaders find the time to devote to proactive ideas and get their followers to do the same is by developing the courage to say no to urgent but low-payoff tasks. Leaders are the relentless enemies of needlessly bureaucratic, time-consuming processes. They eliminate outmoded or unnecessary procedures and call people to focus their attention squarely on the purpose of the enterprise. Leaders focus instead on the big picture and on the future. I recently provided training for a government agency whose director spent time poring over the long distance telephone charges for each employee in her five regional offices, calculating the average length of each and then calling the employees (long distance) to ask for a justification. This type of activity is wholly inappropriate for a person at that level. It transforms the leader into a clerk. And it robs her of the time to create a more positive future for the organization.

Success in leadership, then, requires the capacity to have a dream or a vision of a positive difference one wants to make and the capacity to find and devote the necessary time to turn that vision into a reality. Moreover, by involving their followers in developing proactive ideas, by giving them a sense of purpose and achievement, leaders unleash tremendous motivation inside the organization.

Dealing with Higher Authority

Almost all leaders report to someone else, a senior manager, a board of directors, or an elected official. As mentioned earlier, such people may feel threatened by a leader's bold new approaches. They may have had a hand in designing the status quo, or they are comforted by the fact that the status quo is familiar to everyone in the organization. A change always brings the risk that things might get worse. Elected chief executives are particularly prone to this last fear. That is why, in many agencies, reorganization plans, policy initiatives, and new program planning screech to a halt in election years.

Convincing higher authority of the desirability of change is rarely easy. Many months of effort may be involved, and a leader's idea may be rejected several times before it is finally adopted. However, true leaders persist in this struggle because they have a deep belief in what they are doing; they love their life's work. While others say, "I can't do that because of the policy," leaders take their crusade to the policy-making authority and eventually get the policy changed.

Most often, the reasons advanced for resistance to change are excuses to cover the fact that people are uncomfortable with change. They will not make a change until they can envision a better situation. Therefore, the best way to handle such resistance is to involve higher-level people in the generation of the ideas themselves. In nonprofit agencies, boards should always be involved in the generation of new directions. Leaders should maintain close contact with elected officials, keeping them abreast of what is going on and bringing alive a vision of a better future.

The best way to gain the support of higher authority for a new idea is to get a commitment to improvement in general. Ask those in higher authority whether they think the organization can be improved. Sound these people out for their own ideas. Then ask whether they would be interested in some fresh ideas to make the organization even more effective than it already is. If the people in higher authority are resistant to the very idea of improvement, you are probably working for a dying organization. As a leader, you will only be frustrated in such an environment. Go find a situation in which your talents can find fertile soil.

The Goal of Leadership

Leaders in modern organizations influence others to *want* to follow. They do this by creating an organizational situation in which committed, self-confident people work in exciting jobs that enhance the followers' self-esteem. This is the role of leaders and the goal that should drive leadership behavior. The goal contains four key elements that we will explore in detail—creating commitment, creating self-confidence, creating exciting jobs, and creating self-esteem. It should be noted here that although this book explores these elements individually, they are interdependent and the leadership behavior that produces one element often produces others at the same time. Before we go on to explore these elements, however, let's look at how leaders acquire the ability to influence others to follow.

Chapter Two

Leading Through Status-Based Sources of Power

Leadership, as noted earlier, is the act of influencing others to follow. Leaders work by influence. They act in ways that cause others to choose to act in accordance with their leader's wishes. Since power is the ability to influence the actions of others, leadership can be viewed as the effective use of power. Leaders, therefore, are people who have and use power. This power or ability to influence stems from two broad sources, the position the leader holds and the personal respect that the leader generates from the followers. The power that derives from the former we will call status-related power, whereas that which derives from the latter we will refer to as personal power. Effective leaders know how to use both types of power.

A person who holds a position of authority automatically gains some influence over the people who are subject to that authority. This power stems wholly from the leader's status and has nothing to do with the leader's personality or with whether the followers like the leader. Paul Hersey (1984) distinguishes four levers of such power:

1. The leader controls the rewards the organization can bestow upon the followers.
2. The leader has access to and a relationship with those in higher levels of authority and power.
3. The leader has the ability to punish subordinates.
4. People often have respect for the position itself regardless of who holds it.

Influence from Providing Rewards

When we speak of rewards, many people think immediately of money. In nonprofit and government organizations, there are usually strict limits on using money as a reward, but there are other ways in which leaders can reward people, ranging from praising them to allowing them to work on new projects to giving them tokens of appreciation, such as flowers, cups, or letters. Such psychic rewards meet a person's need for recognition.

Individuals need to feel that the efforts they expend are valuable. They want to feel that what they have done is important. For most people, self-satisfaction in this area is not enough. They need to hear of someone else's satisfaction with their work, preferably someone in authority. They are thereby disposed to behave in ways that will elicit their leader's praise. One of the most common complaints I hear from people in groups where leadership is lacking is "They don't know what I do or care what I do or value my work." To avoid such sentiments, leaders make sure that every group member knows that his or her efforts are recognized and appreciated—in short, rewarded.

The first rule regarding recognition is "give recognition or else." Recognition is one of the most fundamental motivational needs of followers. If they do not get recognition from their leader for productive effort, they may get recognition from their peers for destructive acts. A truck driver in city government, for example, wanted Thursday and Friday off so that she could join her husband on a business trip. Because she had used up her annual leave, her supervisor told her she could not have the time off even without pay, emphasizing that it was against city policy. The city did have a policy, however, that any truck driver who had an accident while backing up would receive an automatic and immediate two-day suspension without pay. On Wednesday afternoon this driver backed her truck into her supervisor's vehicle. Her co-workers, seeing the supervisor stand helpless in rage, gave the driver a standing ovation, thus rewarding her for this act.

The second rule of recognition is that it must be given frequently. Recognition is a motivator of short duration. When I tell a supervisor that her people feel she doesn't value their work, she is often surprised and sometimes incredulous because she can remember expressing her appreciation. "Gee, only two months ago, I told the team that they did the best job I'd ever seen done. How can they feel that I don't appreciate their work?" Effective leaders are in the habit of giving frequent praise and so avoid this problem.

The third rule is that the recognition must be varied. Fortunately, there are hundreds of ways to let people know that their efforts are appreciated. Among the daily means of providing recognition are the following:

> Saying "Thank you"
> Telling them they did a good job
> Suggesting they join you for coffee
> Asking for their opinions
> Greeting them when they arrive in the morning
> Showing interest in their personal interests
> Smiling when you see them
> Bragging about them to your boss (in their presence)
> Writing short thank-you notes to them
> Saying something positive about their personal qualities

Less frequent ways of showing recognition and appreciation to subordinates include the following:

> Taking them to lunch
> Letting them put their names on the products they produce
> Buying the first pitcher of beer for "the best crew of the month"

Writing them a letter of commendation (with copies to their personnel files and all appropriate people)

Putting them on important task forces

Giving the best parking space to the "employee of the month"

Posting graphic displays that show progress toward goals

Mentioning major contributors by name in your status reports to upper management

Arranging for them to present their results to higher-ups

Giving them permission to attend a seminar, convention, or professional meeting, at the organization's expense if possible

Writing articles about their performance

Having them present a training session to co-workers

Celebrating their birthdays

Asking your boss to write them a letter of thanks

Having them represent you at important meetings

Sending letters of thanks to their families when they have been working long hours

Providing recognition or rewards for significant achievements might include one or more of the following:

Having special caps, shirts, belt buckles, or pins made to honor the group

Encouraging them to write an article about an important accomplishment at work

Awarding a plaque, certificate, or trophy to the best employee, best crew, most improved team, or the like

Giving them a raise

Giving them a bigger office

Buying them first-class equipment

Getting their picture in the newspaper

Giving them additional responsibilities and a new title

Putting up a banner celebrating a major accomplishment

Honoring them for years of service to the organization

The fourth rule of recognition is that it must be honest. While it is important to make sure that all are praised for their good efforts, it is disastrous to praise a person for mediocre work. When people are praised for work they know is not their best, they will be forced to conclude that the leader doesn't know the difference between excellent and mediocre work or that the leader is trying to manipulate them. To build commitment, a leader must be seen as trustworthy, not manipulative. Moreover, if the leader gives rewards for mediocre performance, the value that others will place on the recognition they receive will go down. For rewards to produce influence, they must require some effort to earn them. If the leader, in trying to become popular, cheapens the value of the rewards by giving them out too freely, the process will backfire, and the leader may be left feeling that the ungrateful followers have turned against her despite all that she has done for them. Praise only deserving work.

Sometimes people see a contradiction between this rule and the second rule, give recognition frequently. Occasionally, a leader may inherit an employee who doesn't seem to do anything deserving of recognition. In this case, it is important to watch the person closely, to look for anything positive. Despite the leader's low expectations, the person probably does do some things well, and it is important that the leader spot these, no matter how small, and praise them. "You were very pleasant to that client on the phone," for example. This may be the first deserving praise the person has received in years. If he is praised a few more times, he may start to expend more effort in other areas to get additional recognition. From such small beginnings, the leader may eventually turn the person's life around. This is what transformational leadership is all about.

The fifth rule of recognition is that the reward should be given to the person, not to the work. This is a subtle but important point. A few years ago, for example, I spoke at a conference in Saskatchewan that had been organized by a group of volunteers. During the plenary sessions, several speakers publicly praised how well organized the conference was without once mentioning the people who did the organizing. As a result, each statement of praise produced frustration and resentment among the volunteers.

The sixth rule of recognition is that the reward should be appropriate to the achievement. Extraordinary efforts should draw more than a simple thank-you. Small successes should not rate banners and plaques. The foregoing lists of ideas for types of recognition can be used as a guide in adhering to this rule.

Seventh, the recognition should be consistent. If one volunteer or paid staff member is praised for a certain accomplishment, another person should receive similar praise for a similar accomplishment. Many leaders fail here and arouse feelings of favoritism among their people. This tends to produce animosity among employees, making teamwork impossible. A person who feels animosity toward co-workers puts self-interest above commitment to common goals and is far more difficult to influence than a person who feels part of the team.

Eighth, the recognition must be timely. In one agency, for example, a volunteer was applauded at a meeting for an effort she had made two months earlier. This was the first time she had received any praise for her effort, and during the preceding two months, she had resented the lack of appreciation. When the praise did come, its effect was too small to overcome the two months of resentment.

The ninth recognition rule is that the reward should be individualized as much as possible. Just as one person may hate a present that another would love, so recognition must be tailored to the individual's taste. I have a friend who will do practically anything if he knows there is a certificate to be had for doing it. This is readily apparent because his wall is covered with certificates he has received for various achievements, large and small. Others regard certificates as just more pieces of paper to clutter their office. One person may love flowers, another may regard them as sophomoric, and still another may be allergic to them. All of this means that leaders need to know their people well enough to select the appropriate gesture.

The tenth and last rule of recognition is a summary one: pay attention to whatever you want more of. Although this may sound simple, many in leadership positions wind up doing the opposite. They ignore their top performers, glad that they don't have to spend their precious time on these people, and instead devote copious amounts of time and attention to the poor performers, coaching, cajoling, and trying to be viewed as a nice person. All that usually

happens in such scenarios is that the top performers feel unappreciated and get discouraged and the poor performers wind up filing
a grievance against the leader anyway. Attention is a primary need
of most people. Leaders encourage them to earn it through productive activity.

Recognition, in the form of various kinds of rewards, makes
people feel good about their efforts. It develops self-esteem and encourages commitment. It also provides the leader with influence by
creating a sense of obligation in the person who receives the reward.
Giving rewards is thus a synergistic process. It tends to produce
reciprocal behavior, which in turn warrants further rewards.

Influence from Having Connections

A second source of status-related power is the access the leader has
to those with greater status-related power, those in higher authority—for instance, a board of directors or a chief executive. Leaders
who have the confidence and support of those above them will
usually have more influence on their followers than those who do
not enjoy such higher-level support.

Effective leaders are therefore also effective followers. They
make sure that their supervisor or board is kept advised of what they
are doing and the reasons for it. They also make sure that their goals
and the direction in which they are leading the group are approved
by higher authority. Moreover, leaders' actions should be in accordance with the values and standards of that higher authority. If a
leader considers such values and standards to be abhorrent, she or
he should find another group to lead in another organization.

A common failing in this regard comes from a leader's desire
to be liked by her people. As a result, a leader may be tempted to
commiserate with followers about the adverse effects of a decision
of someone in higher authority. "Yes, he sure blew it on that one,
didn't he? I don't know how he could have made such a stupid
decision." Playing "ain't it awful" in this way with followers produces momentary feelings of bonding and a sense that the leader is
succeeding in cementing a relationship with them. The problem
with such behavior is that the leader also lets everyone know that
she disagrees with her boss. In the future, when one of her people

is unhappy with one of her decisions, that person will be tempted to go around her to her supervisor. If word gets out, as it usually does, that the leader commiserated with her people about her boss's decision, the boss may be disposed to side with the leader's subordinate. The rest of her people then see that their co-worker has more power than their leader does, and her ability to influence them is greatly reduced.

To avoid such a scenario, effective leaders try to influence their boss's decision before it is made. This requires a relationship of trust between leader and supervisor. Leaders help establish such a relationship by successfully carrying out their responsibilities and demonstrating over time that their judgment is sound.

When you first begin working for a new person, invest in developing trust. Before taking any significant action, discuss it with your boss. If he or she disapproves, suspend, for the time being, your independent thoughts about what the best courses of action might be and try suggesting ways of doing things that you know the boss will like. People tend to have confidence in those who think the way they do, and this will build trust that your thinking is good because it is the kind of thinking your boss does. After several months of this, you can start to recommend your own ideas. Because you will have built trust early in the relationship, your boss will be more likely to take a chance at this point.

In any event, part of your ability to influence will rest on the perception of how much backing you have from your supervisor. Any disagreements you may have should be voiced privately. If the decision you oppose is nonetheless made by your supervisor, it is essential that you play the part of his or her representative when you announce it to your people and communicate it with the same enthusiasm that your supervisor would. Again, if you cannot do this in good conscience, you need to find a different boss.

One of the problems leaders may face in this regard comes from having a weak manager above them. In one large nonprofit organization, for example, a department head reported to a deputy who was not respected by members of any of the departments he supervised. Having his backing would not have enhanced the department head's power. Fortunately, her power was enhanced by having the full backing of the director of the organization. The danger in such a situation arises when one bypasses the immediate supervisor and goes directly to an even higher authority. Such an action would probably be successful but might well leave the immediate supervisor lusting for revenge, a situation that infuses politics into the daily efforts and distracts people from their purpose. In this particular case, the department head conferred with the director on many decisions and ideas but scrupulously kept the deputy informed.

Influence from Taking Disciplinary Action

A third source of status-related power comes from the ability of the leader to coerce others to do things by punishing them if they do not. Using disciplinary action or coercive power effectively is a delicate matter in that using it too much creates fear. Although people will follow a leader out of fear, as Saddam Hussein, Joseph Stalin, and others have brutally shown, it is not a very productive way to build an effective organization. Where the primary motivator is fear, there is little passion for the purpose of the enterprise. It leads to a lack of risk taking and refuge in the safety of yesterday's procedures, a situation that makes movement toward a better future impossible. Where movement is impossible, leadership itself becomes impossible, because one cannot follow a person who is standing still.

A young executive director of a national organization was concerned that her people be impressed that she was "as hard-nosed as any man." Every six months or so, she would fire someone for making a small mistake. As a consequence, people were afraid to do anything unless she told them exactly what she wanted done. She wound up burned out because she had to orchestrate everyone's actions. Too much reliance on disciplinary power takes a toll on the leader.

On the other hand, a leader's failure to take disciplinary action against those whose behavior is inappropriate leads to a feeling that the leader does not care about upholding the organization's values and standards. Those who continue to behave appropriately in the face of this will tend to resent the leader for not enforcing the values and will not respect or be influenced by the leader.

In the nonprofit world, many leaders have a hard time taking coercive action. When people act unacceptably, these leaders tend to respond by cajoling, counseling, listening, and trying to understand. This tendency comes from the fact that they got into the nonprofit business because they care about people. They don't like to do something unpleasant to another person. When leaders allow inappropriate or irresponsible behavior, however, they cheapen the organization's sense of identity, reducing the sense of commitment of their followers. The followers may continue to perform well out of a sense of personal pride, but they may start looking around for a different job.

The appropriate use of coercive power was demonstrated by a new fire chief in the state of Washington who followed a chief who had the reputation of being "a real nice guy." He had engendered little respect in the employees, however, and discipline was very lax. For instance, the station looked more like a college dorm than the usual fire station. During the new chief's first week, a fire fighter promised a Brownie leader that he would come in on his day off and give the girls in her troop a tour of the fire station. When they arrived, however, the fire fighter was not present. The next day, the chief told the fire fighter that he was going to put a letter of reprimand in the fire fighter's personnel file for not fulfilling a responsibility. The fire fighter complained loudly. The chief listened. When the fire fighter was finished, the chief said, "You know, things are pretty lax around here. You aren't the only one who has failed to fulfill his responsibility. And if word got out that you had received this letter of reprimand, it might be a good thing."

The fire fighter looked down at his shoes for a moment. "Yeah," he said. "I guess it might be worth it then." Then he looked up. "If I did something on my own initiative that was really good, would you consider taking the reprimand out of my file?" he asked.

The chief smiled and replied, "I might be persuaded to do something like that."

The next day, the fire fighter and one of his friends washed and waxed the main fire engine. When the next shift came on duty, they were astonished by the gleaming engine. This encouraged them to clean other pieces of equipment. Because of the new chief's judicious use of the power to discipline, the members began to take more pride in their organization.

Disciplinary action is one of the tools the leader can use to focus people on the right things. It can also have the opposite effect, however. In a state police department, for example, an officer was involved in a high-speed chase. As he drove down the freeway, the driver of the car ahead of him fired several shots at the officer. Eventually, they turned off the freeway onto a country road. When the road came to a dead end, the driver got out and ran across a field. The officer gave chase on foot until they reached a river. The suspect dived in and began to swim across the river. The officer took off his hat and gun belt and swam after the fleeing man, finally catching him on the opposite bank. The officer was reprimanded for not taking his boots off before swimming across the river.

Disciplinary procedures such as this one focus people on the wrong things. They come from people having goals that emphasize the internal workings of the organization rather than the purpose of the agency. They make following procedures more important than achieving the purpose of the organization. A leader in this particular situation could refocus the police force's attention on the department's purpose by reprimanding the sergeant who reprimanded the officer and then congratulating the officer for a job well done in apprehending the suspect.

Influence from Holding the Position

The fourth source of status-related power stems from the followers' respect for the leader's position itself. Most people are disposed to be influenced by someone in a position of authority. The person acquiring the position is given a certain amount of influence simply because she or he holds it. This is particularly true of those who seek to hold the position themselves one day. They want the position to have a certain luster and inherent power. It is the reason they value the position, and it is something to which they can aspire.

An obvious example of this source of influence can be witnessed every year when the president of the United States gives the State of the Union message to Congress. When the president is introduced, a prolonged, enthusiastic, standing ovation is given, even by those who oppose the president's policies and political agenda. It is the position that is being applauded, not the person.

A common failing of leaders, particularly those in human services, is the stripping of status from the leadership position. People new to leadership may feel uncomfortable in the role and therefore seek the familiarity of a nonleadership role. They may feel that the status of their position creates a personal barrier between them and the group they are leading. Too often, new leaders deal with their personal discomfort by trying to make themselves the equals of their followers by stressing that there is nothing special about themselves. To be liked, they may give up certain privileges, such as occupying the best office. By removing the status from their position, however, they remove one source of their influence over the people they must lead and make their success more difficult.

Abraham Zaleznik (1990, p. 79) was one of the first to describe the problem of trying to be liked by stripping the status from the position:

> These attempts . . . fail sooner or later. The executive may discover that his subordinates join in gleefully by stripping his status and authority to the point where he becomes immobilized; is prevented from making decisions; is faced with the prospect of every issue from the most trivial to the most significant being dealt with in the same serious vein. . . . Much to his horror he finds that attempts to remove social distance in the interests of likability have not only reduced work effectiveness, but have resulted in an abortion of the intent to which his behavior has been addressed. He discovers that his subordinates gradually come to harbor deep and unspoken feelings of contempt toward him, because he inadvertently has provided them with a negative picture of what rewards await them for achievement.

As Zaleznik points out, people would rather work for someone who has high status than for someone who has little. When a museum staff moved to a new building, the museum editor complained to her boss about her new work space. The boss offered to trade offices with the editor, giving her a spacious office with a nice view. To the boss's surprise, the editor seemed even more upset by that idea. "That just wouldn't be right" was her response.

Retaining Influence

Although all four of the levers of status-related power that we have examined in this chapter are inherent in the leadership position, they can be lost if they are not used. It is therefore important that those in leadership positions reward positive actions, build strong relationships with those in positions of higher authority, have the courage to punish those whose behavior is inappropriate, and maintain and enhance their followers' respect for the position itself. Leaders who do not use these levers of status-related power will most often lose the respect of their followers and therefore the ability to lead and to influence. And when followers decide not to be influenced, leadership, by definition, becomes impossible.

The old adage about physical fitness thus applies to power—use it or lose it—and the more you use it, the more you will have. The four levers of status-related power are synergistic. For example, upper management is more likely to delegate authority to leaders who have proved that they have the respect of their people. This in turn enables them to control more rewards, which results in stronger allegiance from their people and thus encourages more confidence from those above.

Leaders inherit different motivational situations. Sometimes a leader is lucky enough to follow someone who left behind a situation in which people are committed, self-confident, and capable. In other cases, however, a leader may find that the predecessor was not so adept and the work force unmotivated, incompetent, or both. In the latter situation, leaders may initially have to rely heavily on disciplinary power as they begin to build an effective organization. Meanwhile, they should give recognition where appropriate to begin humanizing the environment and maintain the status and authority of their position while building strong relationships with those in higher authority.

Chapter Three

===============

Developing
Personal Sources
of Power

In addition to the status-related power discussed in Chapter Two, leaders also possess personal power. This does not mean that all leaders have the same type of personality. Leaders can be extroverted or introverted, energetic or low-key. All, however, are dedicated and committed to leading, to moving a group toward a better future.

Leaders' personal power stems from six sources:

1. Their reputation in their field
2. Their technical ability
3. The clarity of their personal objectives
4. The value that their followers place on their relationship with them
5. Their ability to communicate effectively with followers
6. The optimism that stems from their self-confidence and self-esteem

Although these five sources or elements are discussed separately, they are closely related. The common thread that ties them together is the admiration that they engender in followers. They make leaders the kind of people that followers want to become.

Reputation

One aspect of personal power is the leader's personal reputation. If the leader has developed a reputation in her field, others will confer upon her a certain respect. Leaders gain a personal reputation by networking with others both inside and outside the organization. They are members of professional organizations, attend and often chair professional meetings, and are active in professional societies. They either create new approaches within their field or keep up with others who do so. Leaders often enhance their personal reputation by writing articles for professional journals or by serving as speakers at relevant conferences.

This kind of power is not necessarily related to the leader's technical competence. A leader in one nonprofit organization with which I worked built a positive personal reputation by devoting time and energy to strengthening the national professional association in her field. This, in turn, led to her becoming president of an advisory board for a federal agency that granted money to organizations such as hers. Her opinion on a grant application to this agency would guarantee its approval or rejection. As a consequence, she exerted a daily influence on the people in her own organization.

Within an organization, it is the proactive individual who builds a strong personal reputation. As noted in Chapter One, reactive people do only what is required or expected and hence are unremarkable. Proactive people, on the other hand, go beyond the normal expectation of their job requirements and so get noticed. When they succeed in improving the services of the organization or the way in which those services are delivered, they build a reputation. Positive reputations are built from positive achievements, from being "the one" who made something happen. "She's the one who developed that program." "He's the one who automated our procedures." "She's the one who managed to get us some uninterrupted time." These are the kinds of things that are said of budding leaders.

Ability

Leaders also derive personal power from their skills or knowledge in a particular area. Technical or hands-on expertise gives a leader influence over those who have less expertise. When followers need and want information the leader has, they see the leader as someone who can help them succeed in their work. When they need and want skills the leader possesses, they view the leader as someone who can help them grow in their abilities.

Leaders constantly strive to broaden and strengthen their technical ability. They gain new knowledge by reading, attending seminars, and taking college courses. They apply this knowledge in their own work and can be relied upon to help their people solve problems and meet new challenges.

Sometimes people in leadership positions stagnate, or cease to keep up with either their technical field or new developments in management. Often this comes from a fear that if they put themselves in a position of learning, someone will realize that they don't know everything and lose confidence in them. Gradually, the ability of such people begins to erode. Their information and skills are no longer up-to-date. Eventually, the fear that prevented them from learning in the first place is realized and they lose this source of personal power. To keep it, leaders must keep growing. They retain their ability only if they never stop learning.

In addition to increasing their knowledge in their own particular field, leaders often enhance their creativity and value as a resource for followers by keeping abreast of developments in other fields. This enables them to approach problems with a broader perspective and to generate new solutions and new ways of thinking about the organization. Government managers, for example, may subscribe to the *Harvard Business Review*, even though its articles are usually directed to the world of competitive business. Or leaders in human services may regularly read *Scientific American*. Even though the information they glean from such sources may have little direct application, leaders may find new constructs or new, unexpected facts that stimulate their creative thinking. The "breakthrough" ideas that result are frequently impressive to followers and enhance their confidence that these leaders are guiding them in important new directions.

Objectives

Perhaps the most common source of personal power that leaders exert derives from having a sense of direction. A person who has no particular goals in life or who is tentative about his or her own objectives is likely to spend a good deal of time changing direction and spinning his or her wheels. Such a person is not likely to inspire much confidence from others. People tend to respond positively to someone with a clear sense of direction and a strongly internalized purpose. In order to lead, one must have a firm sense of identity and a burning desire to accomplish something specific.

The ability to influence others thus starts with an ability to influence oneself. It begins with quiet self-assessment of where one wants to go and what impact one wants to make, with setting clear goals that fuel one's desire to succeed. One major difference between people who succeed and those who fail as leaders is that the former set goals they can be passionate about. As Anthony Robbins (1991, p. 284) points out, people who have goals that do not inspire them take only lackadaisical action. "The reason is that they're lacking the drive that only a compelling future can provide."

It is surprising how many people seek to succeed in a profession that they don't really like, that they can barely endure. Without a love for what they do, people find it difficult to exhibit the determination, persistence, and commitment that leaders display. Without these qualities, people tend to give up in the face of adversity. Leaders succeed because they keep trying when they encounter setbacks. As long as one is still trying, one has not yet failed. Giving up is thus the only way to fail.

Relationships

A fourth source of personal power comes from the value that followers place on the relationship they have with their leaders. This does not mean that leaders are only concerned about being liked by their followers. Rather, effective leaders require followers to work hard to gain their approval. Once this is attained, it will be valued because it was difficult to earn. It gives followers something to defend.

Leaders enhance this source of personal power by trying to make each interaction with their people a positive one. They find the good in people and praise it. When someone does something wrong, leaders tell that person what to do next time rather than dwelling on past mistakes. Positive statements about another person's qualities are called validations. They differ from recognition in that recognition is given for a particular act while a validation is given for being a certain kind of person. In giving recognition, the leader says, "You did a good job on this." In validating, the leader says, "I am impressed by your abilities." Through validation, leaders make others feel good. This is discussed further in Chapter Nine.

Leaders build relationships by making other people feel welcome, valued, and cared about. They show interest in their people, ask questions about what they care about, try always to offer the first greeting, and listen to their ideas, even if they seem unworkable at first. Leaders call their followers by name, compliment them, remember their birthdays, and most important of all, share the credit with them.

Communication

Throughout history, individuals have influenced groups by powerfully communicating a belief the group already held. Patrick Henry, for example, inspired a nation with his liberty-or-death speech by articulating in a compelling way a yearning for freedom that the majority already shared. People follow leaders readily when the leader articulates a message the followers want to hear.

In organizations, this means that leaders must listen to their people. They must hear their dreams and aspirations. They must find out what people would like their work to mean to them. They must then communicate the purpose of the organization to people in a compelling and powerful way. As we will see in the next chapter, they do this by focusing on the need the organization meets for the people it serves.

Positive Self-Image

Perhaps the most important source of a leader's personal power is a positive self-image. An effective leader has both self-confidence (an optimistic belief in his or her ability to succeed) and self-esteem (a sense of his or her value as a human being). This source of personal power is critical because it is impossible to influence people who do not have confidence in you, and it is difficult to inspire confidence in others if you do not have confidence in yourself. Chapter Nine explores self-esteem in more detail, particularly how leaders build self-esteem in others. Here, we will concentrate on steps leaders can take to build their own self-confidence and self-esteem.

When children are born, they have all the potential in the world to be successful leaders. The fact that so few actually grow up to act as effective leaders is in part due to the fact that something happens to them along the way—they "learn" that they are not the sort of people who exhibit leadership characteristics. This sense of who we are is the most important thing that each of us learns as a child. It forms our psychological gyroscope. It gives each of us a personality, a character, a consistency in our behavior. It develops and evolves in our subconscious mind, without much logical input, long before we have the ability to explore what our true potential is.

Leaders are people who either were taught or discovered early in life the personal qualities that gave them the ability to lead. As Kouzes and Posner (1989, p. 124) point out, "Leaders of the very young, real leaders—those who are naturally followed—are not the hitters, scratchers, pinchers, biters, and pullers. The natural leaders are those who offer toys to others, lightly touch or caress, clap hands, smile, extend a hand." By finding out that this "works" for them, such people develop the personal qualities that serve them as leaders later in life and develop the positive self-image necessary to success in that role. Such a self-image is promoted by a number of factors, including positive self-talk, positive imaging, and an upbeat view of life.

Self-Talk

The term *self-talk* refers to the things we say to ourselves about ourselves. Successful people's self-talk reinforces their success. Obviously, however, self-talk is not always positive, because people tend to be their own harshest critics. One of the business world's most successful leaders is a man named Art Williams (1988) who founded a highly successful insurance company. He is a master motivator and tries always "to be up." Yet he says he has one unachieved goal in life: getting through a single day without hearing any negative self-talk (p. 164).

People's self-talk tends to be a reflection of their beliefs about themselves. For example, saying "I never can find anything" is reflective of a belief that one is disorganized. Such statements also reinforce the belief as being true, exaggerate the frustration, and therefore increase one's negative feelings about oneself.

Affirmations. Although all of us will hear negative self-talk in our minds from time to time, we can do something to limit its impact on our self-confidence and hence on our personal power. Statements known as affirmations can reinforce our positive qualities. To be effective, these statements follow certain rules:

> They are stated in the present tense.
> They are stated in positive terms.
> They are specific, not vague or general.
> They focus on the end result or quality, not on the way in which it will be achieved or developed.
> They have an emotional impact.
> They are stated in simple language.

In terms of the first two rules, saying "I am an optimistic person" is much more effective than saying "I will be optimistic someday." Similarly, saying "I always look on the bright side" (rather than "I am never discouraged") emphasizes the positive quality you want to affirm.

The remaining rules are desirable but not critical. For instance, in terms of the third rule, something vague such as "I have a good personality" is a fine thing to say to yourself, but saying "I am a good listener" or "I care about other people" is more effective because it is more specific. Similarly, there is nothing wrong with saying "I run three miles every morning," but that is an affirmation of a fact rather than of a quality. The statement "I keep myself in good physical condition" affirms a personal quality and so is more likely to reinforce positive, confident feelings about the self.

The last two rules are designed to increase the likelihood that the affirmation will have an effect on our subconscious mind, where our self-image really resides. The subconscious is more susceptible to emotional statements than to long and complex logical concepts. Following are some examples that reinforce personal power.

> I radiate strength and confidence to all around me.
> When the pressure is on, I perform well.
> In the face of adversity, I keep trying until I succeed.
> In difficult situations, my heart fills with confidence and I succeed.
> In the company of others, I feel comfortable, relaxed, and valued.
> People naturally look to me for direction and ideas.
> I make others feel important and capable.
> I always bring out the best in other people.
> I put all my energy into my interactions with others.
> I am a very enthusiastic person.
> Other people enjoy my high energy level.
> When it is time to perform, I always feel great.

In general, affirmations can be formed by putting "I am" or "I always" or "I do" or "I can" or "I'm the kind" in front of any appropriate positive quality. Here are some examples that affirm the quality of being proactive:

> I am a proactive person.
> I always work on proactive tasks first.
> I do things that others only talk about.
> I am the kind of person who takes charge of her life.

The experience of forming such affirming statements may bring to mind others that do not begin with the foregoing phrases but nonetheless follow the rules. For example:

> While others sit and wait, I make things happen.
> I have the courage to act on my own.
> I make dreams come true.
> I love the power of getting things done.

We all have the power to control the thoughts in our heads, although most of us never bother to develop and use that power. If we get in the habit of monitoring our self-talk, we can stop ourselves when we hear negative statements and then replace them with positive self-talk. For example, suppose you forgot an appointment with your supervisor. An hour late, you suddenly remember it and say to yourself, "You jerk. How could you be so stupid? Why do you always screw everything up?" If you are in the habit of monitoring your self-talk, you will say to yourself, "Wait a minute. That's not like me. Other people can count on me. I made a mistake in this one case, but I am a responsible person." You will then feel better and stop reinforcing the negative belief.

In addition to using affirmations as an antidote to negative self-talk, you can use them at any time to enhance your mood. When you are waiting in line or stuck in traffic, seize the opportunity and say something positive to yourself. You might even record some of your affirmations and play them back while you are driving or getting ready for work in the morning. By deliberately repeating positive statements to yourself, you will feel better and also reduce or eliminate negative self-talk.

For leaders, the most important use of affirmations is to enhance their sense of optimism about life. In his book *Learned Optimism*, Martin Seligman (1991) indicates that people are more likely to follow optimistic leaders than pessimistic ones. He identifies six major differences in the self-talk of optimists, who feel in control, and pessimists, who feel helpless.

1. Optimists view positive events as being caused by themselves, while pessimists view them as caused by good fortune or external forces. For example, optimists will say, "I submitted this

legislation at the perfect time," while pessimists will say, "The budget people knew the economy was about to turn around and gave me good advice."

2. Conversely, optimists view misfortune as caused by external sources; pessimists view it as caused by themselves. An optimist, having failed at something, will say, "The task was difficult," whereas a pessimist will say, "I don't have enough talent."

3. Optimists view positive situations as likely to last; pessimists view them as temporary. When someone in higher authority approves a new idea, for example, an optimist will say, "The boss always likes my ideas," while a pessimist will say, "My boss was in a good mood today."

4. On the other hand, optimists view setbacks as temporary, while pessimists tend to regard them as permanent. When a plan doesn't work out, an optimist will say, "I didn't monitor things well enough to make the necessary adjustments in the plan"; a pessimist will say, "Planning is a waste of time," or "My career is finished."

5. Optimists view good events as resulting from general or universal causes, while pessimists view them as specific. When an optimist solves a problem, she will say, "I am good at problem solving." A pessimist will say, "At least I did a good job on that problem."

6. Optimists view difficulty as resulting from specific causes, while pessimists view it as general. A frustrated pessimist, for example, might say, "It's impossible to get anything done in government," while an optimist will say, "It's difficult to get anything done with our procedures the way they are."

Leaders focus on the future, a better future. They must be optimists to keep hope alive in their people. Leaders' self-talk with respect to fortune and misfortune is therefore very important, because it is difficult to keep others up if you are not optimistic yourself. Also, in times of stress, we tend to voice our self-talk to others. Saying something pessimistic such as "We never should have tried this" is not likely to build the confidence of your people.

As Seligman (1991, p. 48) notes, "Finding temporary and specific causes for misfortune is the art of hope: Temporary causes limit helplessness in time, and specific causes limit helplessness to the original situation. On the other hand, permanent causes produce helplessness far into the future, and universal causes spread helplessness through all your endeavors."

Empowering Questions. Affirmations are most effective in supporting beliefs that we already hold about ourselves in times when that quality is challenged by others or in response to our behaving in a manner that is indeed unlike us. They are not, however, particularly effective in overcoming a well-established negative belief about our qualities. If we are deeply depressed, for example, simply repeating to ourselves "I am happy" or "I always respond with enthusiasm to the events of the day" is unlikely to make a big difference, though it may have a temporary effect. A more effective type of self-talk for improving self-confidence is empowering questions.

In our self-talk, we hear questions all the time. These questions can be of two types, empowering or diminishing. Diminishing questions reduce our sense of being in control of our lives. Anthony Robbins offers some common examples of such questions in his book *Awaken the Giant Within* (1991, pp. 190–208).

> Why can't I ever succeed?
> Why is life so unfair?
> Why don't I ever get a break?
> Why am I so depressed?
> How could he (she) do this to me?
> Why do I always sabotage myself?

When we ask these kinds of questions, we are putting ourselves in a very reactive and helpless role. We cast ourselves in the role of a victim of forces larger than ourselves and focus on the negative and pessimistic. We reduce our personal power because although pessimists sometimes attract a following of fellow victims, effective people are generally more prone to follow optimists.

Moreover, when we ask ourselves diminishing questions, we assume that there is something wrong with us and concentrate our energy on finding a rationale for lack of success, thus lowering our self-esteem. If we ask, for example, "Why don't I ever have any luck?" we may conclude, "Because I'm incapable" or "Because other people take unfair advantage of me." Such answers tend to become the basis of beliefs about ourselves. In the above example, the belief that "I am incapable" is a direct consequence of the question "Why don't I have any luck?" This belief is then reinforced in our self-talk, reducing our confidence and self-esteem even further.

Diminishing questions have a direct effect on our mood by causing us to focus on what we cannot control in a situation. Asking, "Why can't I?" causes us to find reasons why we can't. If we are bored, unhappy, frustrated, or depressed, we are probably asking ourselves diminishing questions.

Empowering questions, on the other hand, enhance our sense of being in control. Instead of asking, "Why can't I get to work on time?" for instance, we might ask, "What can I do to get to work on time?" This focuses our attention on positive action we can take. It focuses us on what we can control. Similarly, instead of asking, "Why can't I ever get this done right the first time?" it would be more effective to ask, "What can I do to improve my skills in this area?" Such empowering questions enhance our sense of being a person who makes things happen. Here are some examples of empowering questions people can ask themselves to focus on positive action:

What can I do to improve myself today?
What can I do today that will make the most difference?

How can I become better organized?
What can I do to make myself more promotable?
How can I make this task more fun?

What is there about my behavior that causes this person to react in this way?
How could I behave differently to get a more positive response from this person?
What can I learn from the difficult behavior of this person?
What positive thing could I say to this person?

What can I do today to improve my situation?
What can I do to create a positive environment for myself?

What can I look forward to today?
What can I do to make today better than yesterday?

What am I doing and thinking that is making me feel this
    way?
What could I think about and do that would make me feel
    happier?
What's positive in this situation?
How can I turn this setback into something positive?

What can I do to make progress toward my goals today?
How long should this task take?
How can I get uninterrupted time so that I can get this done
    early?

What can I control in this frustrating situation?
What can I do to brighten this other person's day?
Whom have I helped today?
What positive things happened today?
What have I learned today?

It is essential that leaders ask themselves these kinds of empowering questions to remain upbeat and so to set an example of
enthusiastic optimism. Followers will feel more confidence in
themselves if they know that their leaders are confident. Furthermore, it is simply more pleasant to be around a leader who is in a
good mood, who feels in control.

Imaging

Our beliefs about ourselves are in the form of multisensory images,
not just visual ones. We develop these images over the years on the
basis of real and imagined experiences. We can take important steps
to modify and strengthen them by creating our own multisensory,
imaginary experiences.

Years ago, I had a friend named John, who was a high school
music teacher. John had a student in his guitar class who was a
phenomenally quick learner. Every day John would show the stu-

dent some guitar technique and he would try it. By the end of class, he would not be able to do it, but at the beginning of the next class he could perform it perfectly. When John asked him how he managed to do this, the student replied, "Well, you see I sleep with my little brother. Every night when I go to sleep, I have to think of something other than wondering when he will wet the bed. Lately, I've been thinking about that guitar thing you showed me in class. I think about it real hard, so the thought of my brother wetting the bed can't enter my mind. And I think about it and I think about it and I think about it and eventually I can just do it."

Many studies have shown that such vivid imaging is as good as or sometimes superior to actually practicing to acquire a skill. Similarly, if we vividly imagine ourselves behaving with a certain ability, it enables us to experience that as being true. This works because the subconscious mind cannot distinguish the difference between a real event and one that is vividly imagined. To create a vividly imagined scene, we need to make sure that it involves the whole brain, that it is rich in its detail, and that it involves all the senses. It also should inspire the emotions we would feel in a real situation.

To create your own effective multisensory image, first choose a quality or ability you would like to possess. You might choose the quality of self-confidence, for example, or the ability to type rapidly and accurately. Then construct a detailed image that includes the following:

> What you see
> What you touch or feel
> What you hear
> What you smell or taste
> What emotions you experience

Again, make each image component as detailed as possible. If you choose the quality of self-confidence and you imagine yourself presenting an idea to your boss, for example, make sure you really see her in your mind. See loose threads on a button on her jacket, the fine perspiration on her forehead, and so forth. Feel the cushions of the chair in which you are sitting. Hear your own voice speaking with confidence. Taste the coffee she has given you. Feel the emotion of pride you experience as she tells you what a wonderful idea you have.

Once you have created a positive image, you can use it the same way you use positive self-talk. You can dwell on it while driving, exercising, or waiting. You can also use a previously constructed positive image to replace a negative one. Similarly, you can use vivid imaging to supplement practice in acquiring a skill. As the young guitar player learned, you will learn new skills much more quickly if you practice them in your mind between periods of real practice.

One of the most powerful uses of images is to alter one's moods. As noted earlier, it is difficult to remain in a negative mood if you are repeating positive thoughts to yourself. It is even harder to be in a negative mood if you are dwelling on a positive image. If you are spending a precious Saturday cleaning your house and doing laundry, for example, you might find yourself feeling victimized by your no-good, lazy spouse or by your inability to afford a housekeeper. You might ask yourself, "Why do I have to spend my Saturday doing this stuff when other people are out having a good time?" You are feeling frustrated, powerless, and angry at yourself. If you are in the habit of monitoring what goes on in your head, you might stop and realize that you do not have to clean house today. You are choosing to clean house because it is important to you to have pleasant surroundings. You change your sense of not being in control by asking, "How can I do this better than I've ever done it?" or "How can I make this a positive task and an enjoyable experience?" You might then resolve to make the best of the situation by spending this routine time working positively on your self-image. You repeat some affirmations to yourself ("I am a powerful, important person. I am in control of what I do.") and begin to dwell on your positive image.

A strong self-image is, of course, based on real achievement, not merely imaginary adventures. Although we cannot easily do what we cannot imagine and although vivid imaging makes it easier to succeed in the real world, we must eventually try out the imagined behavior if we are to be more than dreamers. If things do not go well when we try out the behavior, we can say to ourselves,

"That's not like me," imagine the success we had in our imaginary experience, and then try again.

Mood Control

Many people think that moods are caused by outside events. Something negative happens to us and we get angry or depressed. They tend to assume that people with positive attitudes are those on whom good fortune has smiled. In fact, however, our moods can be manufactured and controlled.

If you want to feel depressed, for example, you can make it happen by thinking about a time when you hurt another person, by saying to yourself "I have no redeeming value" and by adopting the posture (slumped), facial expression (slack), and behavior (staring blankly, breathing shallowly with occasional sighs) that characterize this emotion. In my seminars, I sometimes ask people to pair off and look at each other. I instruct one member of each pair to feel anger at the other. Most people fail miserably at this and wind up laughing instead, the exact opposite of anger. The point is to demonstrate that it is difficult simply to will an emotion. Some people do, however, manage to succeed in this exercise. When I ask them what they did to conjure up such an emotion, they invariably say that they imagined some past event that made them angry or they imagined that their partner had said something insulting to them. I ask the partners of those people to report what they saw the other person do. Invariably, they report a narrowing of the eyes, a tightening of the mouth, tensing of the hands and shoulders, and a setting of the jaw. By controlling their thoughts and their expression, they managed to bring about the emotion without any external stimulus. This is the essence of imaging.

Our moods are also affected by our self-talk, the body language we use, our diet, and a number of other factors described in the following pages. By controlling these factors we can control our moods and thus develop an enormous reservoir of personal power from which we can draw in the hardest of times.

Psychologist William Glasser (1984, pp. 48–49) explains how emotions are actually chosen:

When I fail a test, the "depression" I feel doesn't happen to me; it is the feeling component of the total behavior of depressing that I am choosing in this unhappy situation. This means that I not only choose to sit in the chair and choose to think miserable thoughts, both obvious choices, I also choose the "depression" I feel and the headache or diarrhea that I "suffer." It is impossible to choose a total behavior and not choose all its components. If, however, we want to change a total behavior, the way we can do it is to choose to change its doing and thinking components.

In the face of adversity, people look to the leader for cues on how to react. If an organization's funding is cut, for example, or a risky venture didn't turn out very well and the newspaper has just published a stinging accounting of the debacle, members of the organization look to the leader for clues as to how to behave. If the leader is depressed or panic-stricken or defeated, if she sits staring at her shoes, saying, "This is a disaster," her followers will also adopt that mood. If the leader is able to control her mood, however, to stay "up" and optimistic and positive, to get people going again, she can be the source of inspiration from which her followers can draw strength in such situations.

The ability to maintain an upbeat mood, to remain optimistic even in the face of adversity, is, of course, not always easy. In addition to organizational difficulties, leaders will no doubt also face personal adversity from time to time. Nevertheless, along with self-talk and imaging, described earlier in this chapter, there are some devices for maintaining optimism when the world around us seems to rock on its foundation.

Body Language. Our feelings are part of a complex of behavior and are manifested in our physical behavior. Angry people, for example, tend to narrow their eyes and tighten their mouths. Depressed people tend to slump, breathe shallowly, and sigh. Much recent research shows that by adopting a certain posture and facial expression, people will start to feel the corresponding emotion.

When you begin to feel angry, frustrated, disgusted, or depressed, try to adopt the posture and facial expression of a person who has just experienced a victory. You will feel better, and others will be able to take this positive cue from you.

Exercise. Effective leaders are usually energetic people. They are able to work hard and to talk with passion about what they do. Mental and physical energy come from our supply of oxygen and glucose. Regular aerobic exercise will help provide an ongoing supply of both fuels.

Diet. What we eat has an effect on how we feel. Because we each have different metabolic reactions to certain foods, it is important to keep track of what we eat and note our mood an hour or two afterward. Experiment. Try things such as the following:

> Eat only fruit during the morning.
> Eat five small meals rather than three large ones each day.
> Don't skip breakfast.
> Drink eight glasses of water a day.
> Make dinner your smallest meal of the day.
> Avoid chocolate for at least a month.
> Eliminate caffeine for at least a month.

Also note your reactions to certain combinations of foods. For example, some people feel more energetic when they do not combine large quantities of proteins and carbohydrates. By paying close attention to what you eat and how you feel afterward, you can design a diet that contributes to your feeling of well-being and confidence.

Doing What You Love. It is much easier to maintain a positive mood when the work we do is something we truly love doing. This naturally endows us with persistence and determination and passion. Soichiro Honda, after a ceremony honoring his contributions to restoring the Japanese economy following World War II, was asked how he found it within himself to keep going in the face of the exacting challenges he faced in his life. He replied, "I don't really find it very exacting because I am doing what I like to do" (Loehr and McLaughlin, 1987, p. 211). If you are not presently working in a field you love, get out while there is still time.

Focusing on Goals. Low emotional ebbs happen rarely to people who are focused on long-term goals; when they do occur, such lows tend to last for relatively short periods of time. It is easier to view adversity as a temporary setback that will be overcome tomorrow if you focus on exciting goals that contribute to an overall optimistic outlook.

Focusing on Learning. Leaders ask everyone (including and especially themselves), "What can we learn from this situation that will make us invincible in the future?" They are in the business of making constant improvements in the way things work, in the business of promoting learning. They encourage people to take reasonable risks and to strive for goals without certainty of success. They react to setbacks and "failure" by asking for learning rather than by laying blame.

In his books and articles, management guru Tom Peters frequently stresses the importance of fast failures, of getting to the failure quickly so that we can learn from it and become wiser than we were before. Equally as important as learning from failure, however, is learning from success. A success we do not learn from is a success that does not strengthen us or the people we wish to lead.

Persistence. What would you attempt if you knew it was impossible to fail? Remember that one never fails until one quits. Abraham Lincoln, for example, never succeeded in winning an office until he ran for president. Had he never run for that office, had he quit politics after Stephen Douglas beat him in a Senate race, Lincoln would have been judged a failure. Most people who succeed do so after persisting in the face of setbacks.

The ability to persist is tied directly to doing what we love and to the degree of optimism we possess. As Martin Seligman (1991) found in his study of pessimism, those with a negative view of the future tend to give up when they encounter a situation in which they lose control. To use an analogy, if we think of our brain as a computer, we are stuck with the computer we have. We can't trade in our nerve cells for a different batch. However, we are not stuck with the software we have acquired along the way. We are not stuck with the habits of thought and emotion that we have adopted to respond to life. All of us have the ability to reprogram our software by means of the devices outlined above. All of us have the potential to possess the positive personal qualities we desire and to achieve the things that people with such qualities achieve, the potential to be leaders.

Situational Uses of Power

So far in this book, we have looked at two kinds of leadership power, the power that stems from the leader's status in the organization and the power that the leader develops personally. Circumstances dictate which kind of power needs to be dominant. Generally, the type of power varies with the motivation and ability of the work force. In this regard we can distinguish four different types of followers:

1. Those who are highly motivated and extremely capable
2. Those who are unmotivated but capable
3. Those who are motivated but not very capable
4. Those who exhibit neither motivation nor ability

The first type of follower is developed through the leadership activities discussed in Chapters Four through Ten of this book. Leaders with such employees rely solely on personal power for their influence. Leaders of the other three types of employees use varying combinations of status-related and personal power.

As noted in Chapter Two, the leader may find that status-related power derived from coercion is necessary to goad people to action when their motivation and ability are low. At the opposite end of the spectrum, with people who are highly motivated and have the ability to fulfill their responsibilities well, the leader relies more on personal power as a source of influence. This type of power stems from the kind of person the leader is and is applied less directly.

Although some aspects of leaders' personal power come from their personal qualities, their magnetism, the quality that unites followers into a committed group, comes more from what leaders do than from who they are, as we will see in the remainder of this book.

PART TWO

BRING OUT THE BEST
IN YOUR ORGANIZATION

Chapter Four

Building Commitment
Through Purpose

In my definition of leadership, I said that leaders create a situation in which committed, self-confident people work in exciting jobs that build their self-esteem. This chapter explores some of the ways in which leaders elicit commitment.

As Abraham Zaleznik (1989) points out in *The Managerial Mystique,* creating commitment is difficult in modern times, when most employees are more committed to their own career advancement than to anything else. When work does not inspire commitment, people work only to make money. They work hard for an organization only until they get a better offer elsewhere. The manager at a Federal Express office in Michigan recently spent $17,000 training one of his people, only to see the person take another job when the training was finished. As we approach the twenty-first century, and labor shortages emerge in many fields and mobility becomes more and more the norm, such occurrences are likely to be increasingly frustrating for organizations.

What Commitment Is Not

The word *commitment* has many connotations, so let us first dwell on what it does not mean in our definition of leadership. Often, the word is used to mean personal loyalty, to imply that followers are willing to stand by the leader under any circumstances. This emphasis on personal loyalty tends to create rival camps among an organization's top managers. It places the emphasis on politics rather than on what the organization exists to achieve. Politics is one of the biggest enemies of an effective organization. Where it is rampant, no leadership is being exercised.

For example, one state employment service department has three assistant directors. One supervises field operations, a network of thirty field offices with three regional directors. The field offices have two main purposes: (1) to handle claims for unemployment insurance and (2) to provide job-finding assistance (employment services). At headquarters, the other two assistant directors function in policy-making roles, one for unemployment insurance and the other for employment services. These two assistant directors also control the purse strings for their respective services. They fund the local offices and tell them how to spend the money, but they have no direct supervisory authority over them.

This cumbersome organizational structure, so typical of government organizations, demands a great deal of communication and cooperation among the three assistant directors. It also, however, is a recipe for conflict. The fact that two of the directors make policy to be followed by people supervised by someone else tends to lead to policies being made without the input of those who have to carry them out. This produces the twin curses of impractical policies and resentment.

In this particular case, the emphasis on personal loyalty in all three divisions of the organization has led to chaos. It has created warring fiefdoms, each with its loyal soldiers, willing to fight for their cause. Field personnel threaten to ignore the policies made without their involvement. In response, they are threatened with loss of funding. The organization thus spends vast amounts of its time on political maneuvering and conflict resolution. Cooperation among the three units, so vital to success, has been replaced with what one staffer calls "cold war negotiations." In this atmosphere, the most important thing is internal politics, not service to unemployed people. As one local officer manager puts it, "It's amazing people get any service at all."

Commitment also does not mean loyalty to the organization. Such an emphasis leads to poor service and obsolescence. On Martin Luther King's birthday in 1990, for example, computer problems made it difficult for AT&T customers to complete long distance calls. Many people asked the AT&T operators whether there were any other ways to complete their calls. Although the operators knew the customers could dial an access number to place their calls with another carrier, their loyalty to AT&T kept them from giving out that information. The next day, newspapers carried the story of this lack of concern for customers. The company not only provided bad service but wound up with a bad reputation as well.

In nonprofit and government organizations, loyalty to the organization often leads staff and volunteers to defend the status quo. When a client or other person makes a suggestion or asks a question such as "Why do I have to give you the same information on two different forms?" a staffer who is loyal to the organization may feel defensive. Rather than considering the opportunity to improve the system for the client, he will instead tend to devote his efforts to developing a justification for the current system. The human mind is a marvelously creative instrument when it comes to justifying the current system, and this tends to lock the organization into the outdated procedures of the past.

What Commitment Is

What commitment does mean in our definition of leadership is a passion for the purpose of the organization. Leaders keep their people focused on the impact the organization is trying to make. In a state department of environmental affairs, for example, leaders keep their group focused on protecting the environment instead of on the process of permit application. In a fire department, they keep the group focused on saving lives and property rather than on meeting the requirements of the drill schedule. In a literacy program, they keep their group focused on helping others learn to read rather than on the procedure for certifying tutors.

Although these may seem like obvious examples, in too many organizations people get so bogged down in the process of doing things that they lose sight of why they are doing them. They get bogged down in petty squabbles about details of the operation, about what office hours to have or on what color paper to print the newsletter. Even where the purpose should seem obvious, people can lose sight of it. In a city fire department, an officer in one company got so bogged down in the routine of drill and rolling up hose that he no longer focused on saving lives and property. In cases where his company and another one were both called on the same emergency, he would say, "Let the other guys handle it" and not respond. Leaders ensure that purpose takes precedence over procedure.

Defining the Mission

The most fundamental way in which leaders create commitment to a purpose is by defining what that purpose is. With the involvement of the people being led, the leader defines the mission of the organization or the unit. The mission is a statement of the purpose of the group being led, a statement of its ultimate goal. When this goal is achieved, the need for the group will no longer exist.

The mission statement should not be contained in some dusty paragraph that is locked away in a drawer, liberated only to preface grant proposals. It should be a statement that galvanizes the followers, a statement from which their daily activities draw meaning. It should be a living declaration of what the group is trying to accomplish. It should be a statement of the difference the group intends to make in the world.

Leaders make sure that the purpose is clearly stated and kept before the group. They also take pains to define a mission that inspires commitment. The mission statement of one small bank was "Our mission is to provide a maximum rate of return to our shareholders." This statement produced a feeling of alienation in the work force. Bank personnel did not find it inspiring to go to work each day knowing that their purpose was to make other, anonymous people rich. At a retreat, the bank managers changed the mission statement to "Our purpose is to provide for the economic well-being of our community through prudent and growth-producing investment that enriches the lives of all citizens." This new mission statement with a focus on the community gave the workers something worth getting excited about. It was a mission that inspired them to work hard.

To be motivating, the mission statement also needs to be as specific as possible. "Our mission is to meet the needs of our clients for human services," for example, does little to fire people up. What are those needs? Why are they important? Leaders make the mission come alive by making the purpose and its importance vivid and concrete: "Our mission is to end the suffering of battered women in our community and build their self-esteem so that they can go on to lead fulfilling and productive lives," for example.

By creating a compelling mission statement, leaders instill a passion for achieving that mission in their people. By instilling such a passion, they create a positive work atmosphere and a desire to succeed that cement teamwork and carry the group past obstacles. People who work for an effective leader love what they do.

A common weakness of organizational mission statements is that they describe what the organization does rather than what it intends to accomplish, that is, what its ultimate purpose is. A literacy program, for example, might talk about providing tutoring services to functionally illiterate adults rather than about putting an end to functional illiteracy in the community. A mission statement such as "We exist to provide hot meals to senior citizens" does not express an ultimate purpose. Mission statements that define what the organization does do not galvanize followers as readily as mission statements that talk about meeting a need. It is boring to prepare and serve hot meals, but it is rewarding to help put an end to senior malnutrition. Mission statements that merely describe what a group does also tend to limit the organization to that activity and to lock people into doing things a certain way because "we've always done them that way." They tend to promote the status quo and so make leadership impossible. No one is leading a group if it is standing still.

The missions of successful organizations, be they businesses, government agencies, or nonprofit agencies, are based on meeting a need. The need the group proposes to meet should ordinarily be one that exists outside of the organization. "We have a problem recruiting volunteers" is not the sort of need we are examining here. In the case of nonprofit organizations involved in direct service activities, the need will be the need of the clients they serve. Following are some examples.

> Youth organization: "Many young people grow up without the skills and self-confidence to become competent, successful adults. Our mission is to equip youth to have a fulfilling, successful life, however they may define it."
>
> Mental health center: "Many people are in doubt, fear, and pain in our community. Our mission is to help them overcome this condition so as to prevent their doing harm to themselves and others and to help them return to independent living as productive members of the community."
>
> Child abuse prevention program: "Our purpose is to stop the cycle of abuse so that all children can grow up in a loving environment that builds their self-esteem."
>
> Community action agency: "Our mission is to help people overcome their poverty and become self-sufficient."
>
> Community volunteer center: "Many people in our community are concerned about community problems but either feel powerless to do anything about them or don't know how to get involved in the solution. At the same time, many agencies in our community are unable to meet fully the needs of their clients because of a lack of personnel. Our mission is to solve both of these problems by providing an avenue for people to get involved in meaningful volunteer work."

The foregoing mission statements are for entire agencies. Individual units of an agency can also have mission statements based on an external need. For example, a state department of wildlife with a mission of maintaining viable populations of native species may have a habitat division whose mission might read: "Essential wildlife habitat is being lost, crowding species into an ever smaller area and placing great stress on the species. Our mission is to ensure the survival of native wildlife by protecting their habitat against the encroachments of developers." The achievement of this unit's mission will make a direct, logical contribution to the agency's overall purpose of protecting all species of native wildlife in the state.

For most organizations, the mission is stated in terms of solving a single problem. Sometimes, however, the organization has more than one purpose, though the purposes may be related. A county surface water department, for example, has a mission statement that says, "Our mission is to protect people from floods while at the same time enhancing the function and protecting the existence of streams, lakes, and wetlands." Although each of these purposes could be achieved without achieving the other, the two have a logical connection.

In some cases, the need that a unit addresses is the need of staff within the organization but outside the unit. A typing pool, for example, might usefully think of the employees who bring it work as its customers. It is the satisfaction of these customers' needs that is the mission of that unit.

By focusing on the need, leaders make it more likely that the group's efforts will have a high payoff. A port community relations group, for example, changed its mission from "shape and communicate port policies to the community" to "create a positive picture of the port in the minds of the community." To accomplish the first mission, all the group had to do was tell people what the port's policies were. If members of the community didn't like the policies, that was too bad. The second mission provided the group with a challenge, with a meaningful goal to accomplish.

The mission statement should be developed with the involvement of the people who will be attempting to carry it out. For nonprofit agency mission statements, this means that the board of directors should involve the paid staff and volunteers. Doing so ensures that they will feel a sense of ownership in the mission. The leader can facilitate this process by asking questions such as "What is our purpose? What is the need in the outside world that we are trying to meet? Under what circumstances could we happily go out of business?" Sometimes, however, boards meekly defer to staff in creating a mission. In doing so, they abdicate their most important leadership role.

Often, a group and its leader assume that the ensuing discussion will take only a few minutes. The mission seems obvious to each person. Invariably, they are surprised, however, to discover that there are small or even major differences in opinion. Many mission-setting meetings turn out to be grueling, frustrating events that last for hours or even days. Nevertheless, the effort is worthwhile because each person is then able to relate his or her beliefs and actions to the ultimate purpose of the organization. This creates meaning in the participants' work lives and is a fundamental component of their motivation and commitment.

Sometimes such discussion of the mission will uncover a deep conflict among members of the group. Where the mission is assumed rather than explicit, this conflict tends to play itself out in petty politics, its roots obscured by the issues of the day. At an art museum, for example, the discussion of the mission uncovered a conflict between the many curators who thought that the mission was to preserve valuable works of art, others who thought the mission should be to provide the public with the works of art they wanted to see, and still others who were adamant that the purpose of the museum was to broaden the taste of the public for all forms of art. Before this discussion occurred, there had been many arguments about the types of exhibitions and programs the museum should sponsor, disagreements that had turned into nasty, personal infighting. As the group discussed the museum's mission, the various factions suddenly understood the source of the conflict and came to understand each other's behavior.

Although it is important for the leader to involve the group in defining its mission, the leader is more than a facilitator of the group's decision making. When members of the group have firm contradictory ideas about the purpose of the organization or when their ideas are unimaginative, inwardly focused, or otherwise unacceptable, the leader must step in and define the purpose.

Where leaders must report to higher authority, such a definition will stick only if they have power, particularly power that stems from their relationship with that authority. Otherwise, members of the group who disagree with the mission may attempt end runs around a leader to his or her boss.

Strategic Planning

The organization's mission statement is applied to individual jobs by means of strategic planning. In this way, the "why" of the mission becomes the "why" behind daily activity.

With the assistance of the group, the leader launches the strategic planning by identifying the obstacles that exist to accomplishing the mission. The overcoming of these obstacles should serve as the major, strategic goals of the group. For example, a volunteer group that works with teenaged drug abusers in a large city identified the following obstacles to overcoming the problem of their drug abuse:

> Peer pressure to use drugs
> Low self-esteem
> Lack of basic skills
> Parental abuse
> Wide availability of drugs
> Belief that drug abuse is harmless
> No sense of a better future
> Lack of alternative recreation

Thus the major strategic goals of this organization became "overcome peer pressure," "improve the teenagers' self-esteem," and so on.

Because some obstacles are insurmountable by any one group, it is best not to waste the group's resources on trying to overcome them, relying on the reduction of other obstacles for progress toward the mission. Rather than trying to overcome the obstacle of the national debt, for example, the group would be better advised to focus its attention on something more tractable.

On the other hand, sometimes obstacles that seem insurmountable, such as peer pressure to use drugs, can in fact be addressed productively, as we will see in a moment. As mentioned in Chapter One, the leader's biggest enemy is the thought that "we couldn't do that." By asking, "How could we do this?" the leader helps people turn in a positive direction. The amount of creativity unleashed in response to such a simple question is often remarkable.

The effective leader also identifies resources in the world outside the group that could help overcome the problem. Mobilizing those outside resources then becomes an additional strategic objective. In the case of teenaged drug abusers, for example, the volunteer group identified the major newspapers of the city as a resource. The leader asked what purpose the newspapers could serve in achieving the mission of overcoming teen drug abuse. The group decided the papers were already doing an adequate job of spreading the news of the negative consequences of drug abuse but were not letting teens know about the successes former drug users were making of their lives. The goal was thus to change teens' attitudes toward former drug users through increased newspaper coverage of such cases.

The next step in creating a mission-based strategic plan is to fix responsibility for achieving the strategic goals, for unless an individual or team is clearly responsible for making progress toward achieving the goals, little is likely to happen. This can be a matter of making the responsibility part of each person's job description, or the leader can ask, "Who will take responsibility for this goal?" or "Which goal would you like to work on?"

The individual or team responsible for a given strategic goal is then asked to develop a strategy for achieving it. For example, the group who took on the (at first) seemingly impossible task of overcoming peer pressure to use drugs decided that the best approach would be to create some positive peer pressure. To do this, it set the goal of establishing an alternative high school for teens who had made a commitment to a drug-free life. Once such a goal is set, the process is one of managing the individual or members of the group as they make progress toward the goal.

Once again, it is important that the leader invite group participation in setting strategic goals to help build feelings of connectedness, identification, and power. As members work on the approved strategy, they then know why they are doing what they are doing and can also relate this to the mission.

Each job in the organization thus acquires a purpose, which

is part of making jobs exciting, a subject that will be covered in more detail in Chapter Six. For now, suffice it to say that every job in an organization should have a clearly stated, overall goal and that if the employee or volunteer makes progress toward that goal, he or she will be making progress toward the achievement of the goals of his or her unit. As the unit makes progress in achieving its goals, the organization makes progress in achieving its mission.

Where jobs are not connected to the purpose, work becomes just something to do. At times it may be interesting or fun, but there is no passion behind it. People begin to wonder why they are doing certain things, and they begin to speculate. Speculations become rumors and rumors become facts in the minds of workers. In one public works department, for example, employees were asked to pave a road that had less traffic than another unpaved road. They asked why they were doing it and were told, "Because the boss wants it done." This being unsatisfactory, one person said, "Maybe one of the commissioners has a relative on this road." By the end of the day, this rumor had become elaborate, and even included the name of a commissioner. The "why" that was created certainly did not produce much enthusiasm or commitment in those who had the job of paving the road. Leaders make sure people don't waste their mental energy on such speculation. They tell their people all relevant facts about the purpose of the work and thus enable them to focus their mental energy on thinking about ways to do the work better.

Keeping the Mission Alive on a Daily Basis

Once people have a sense of direction and job goals related to accomplishing the organization's mission, leaders can keep them on track by making sure that people give top priority each day to the activities that will make progress toward those goals. Leaders do this by keeping the sense of purpose at the forefront of their people's minds.

For example, imagine a state employee who works for the training division of a state department of personnel. The mission of the department is to attract and develop highly motivated and capable people to enable the various other departments of the state to achieve their missions. The mission of the training unit is to maximize the skills of the state employees. The employee is responsible for planning courses that develop skills identified by the various other departments of the state. One day the employee has the following list of things to do:

1. Review an unsolicited proposal from a consultant to conduct a course on internal customer service
2. Respond to a thirteen-page internal departmental questionnaire on employee attitudes, due that day
3. Prepare course descriptions for a request for proposal to independent consultants and trainers
4. Respond to a letter of complaint from an employee about the lack of parking facilities at the training center
5. Respond to a request from a graduate student at a local university that she be allowed to use the unit's data on the effectiveness of training and send it to her for her master's thesis
6. Call the training coordinators in the largest state departments to get their ideas about doing an assessment of management training needs
7. Process a trainer's invoice for a workshop conducted last week
8. Read a new book on management that has just topped the best-seller list
9. Review the evaluations of a new course that was conducted last month

In situations where the sense of purpose is blunted, employees tend to direct their first efforts to the tasks that are most urgent. Accordingly, this employee might spend his time on the questionnaire, the consultant's invoice, the complaint from the trainee, and the graduate student's request. On the other hand, if he and his supervisor have discussed the purpose of his job each month and set short-term objectives in line with that purpose, the employee may have set the following goals for himself: (1) identify management training needs that our courses are not meeting, and (2) develop a new idea for a management training course. In such a circumstance, it is more logical for him to give priority to items six, eight, and nine of the preceding list. His actions are thus channeled toward the mission through a hierarchy of results. The organization's mission provides a purpose that gives meaning to everyone's actions. Without such a sense of direction, leadership is impossible, and the focus of the organization is blurred.

Creating a Vision

Whereas the mission statement is a one-paragraph or one-sentence statement of purpose, of *why* the group exists, the vision is a more detailed statement of *what* the organization will be like in the future.

As for a nation, an organization's success is a consequence of its vision of the future. If that vision is positive, optimistic, and holds forth a better life for the workers and the clients, the organization will succeed. If the vision is one of limits, scarcity of resources, and getting by with less, the organization will not succeed. Unfortunately, too many people in leadership positions pay little heed to this crucial factor. They leave their people to form separate visions of where the organization is going, producing conflict and risking the development of negative pictures. When you leave the vision to chance in this way, you are not leading.

In Chapter One we explored how leaders can unleash the creative ideas of their people in creating a sense of what the organization could become. One potential problem of relying on the ideas of those already connected with the organization, however, is that it encourages thinking about the world inside the organization. To avoid insular thinking, two other approaches can be used. One, pioneered by General Electric in the business world, is to start a "best practices" program. By attending national meetings, leaders can identify similar organizations that are better at certain aspects of operating than they are. They usually visit those organizations with a small team of people who are key players in those particular aspects. The Seattle Art Museum, for example, sent its public relations and publications directors to museums in Chicago, New York, and Atlanta to learn how they obtain publicity and prepare text panels for their exhibits. Upon their return to Seattle, the two directors convened a small task force to explore how to use the information they had gathered to improve the way their museum handled these two areas. The results of such activities can become part of the vision statement.

The second way to avoid an internal focus is to create a vision that is mission focused. Leaders of government and nonprofit organizations (again, with the cooperation of their followers) identify the groups in the community that each organization wants to influence. A systematic way to do this is to list the obstacles the organization faces in accomplishing its mission and the resources (both actual and potential) that could help it move toward the mission. The groups and individuals that show up on this list are people the organization should try to influence. The board and staff of one historical museum, for example, identified the following groups and individuals:

> The county commissioners
> The local newspaper
> Tourists
> People who use the museum for research
> The chamber of commerce
> The city manager
> Local businesss
> A local developer
> The schools

After identifying appropriate groups and individuals, the next task is to ask what the organization wants these people to do for it. In the case of the museum, the answers were as follows:

> The county commissioners give us regular funding and a one-time grant to help purchase a new building.
> The local newspaper gives us coverage of museum events and recognizes our value to the community.
> Researchers write letters of support to funding sources and provide materials to enhance our collection.
> Tourists visit the museum (and pay admission fees), spread positive word about the museum back home, buy things at the gift shop, and buy food in the restaurant.
> The chamber of commerce provides information to members

about museum events and encourages members to support the museum financially.

The city manager provides regular funding.

Local businesses contribute to the building fund and endow chairs.

A local developer donates land downtown for a historic preservation district in which the museum will be built as a replica of an old hotel.

The schools make our educational offerings part of the curriculum, give students credit for volunteering at the museum, and support our funding requests.

These answers created a vision of an ideal environment for the organization. Coupled with the request for proposals from those inside the organization, as described in Chapter One, and the identification of best practices of similar groups, they created a powerful vision of what the museum can strive to become. A vision statement for this historical museum might read as follows:

By the year 1999, the XYZ Historical Museum has moved into a new building, a replica of a turn-of-the-century hotel that was destroyed by fire in 1928. The site was donated by a local developer and features a view of the harbor. The building was paid for by private donations and a grant from county government. Funding for four staff members is secure through an endowment fund and annual budget contributions of local government and the public schools. In addition, grants are received from state sources for special projects and exhibits. The chamber of commerce is active in helping the museum acquire new objects of historical interest. Each year, high school students compete for fifteen volunteer positions, in which they serve in a variety of exciting capacities. The museum is a popular tourist destination, with people coming to see the exhibits, buy gifts, and relax at the cafe. Local residents show off the museum to their visitors. The deck behind the cafe is a popular spot for people to wait for the ferry. Scholars from across the region conduct research in a special room designed for this purpose. Their letters of thanks assist the museum in securing funding for special projects. High school teachers use museum resources to help teach their students local history. The museum is such a popular attraction that it has encouraged local businesses to spring up on the same block, increasing the vitality of the neighborhood.

A vision statement such as this one establishes an ambitious, challenging set of goals for the museum. Although the goals may at first seem daunting, as the museum personnel take small steps toward the realization of the vision, their sense of purpose and excitement grows. They can clearly picture the type of institution they are creating, and that picture gives meaning to their daily actions.

To be effective, of course, the vision statement must be more than merely some writing on a piece of paper. It must live in the hearts of the people who work for the organization. To ensure this, leaders involve as many people as possible in the creation of the vision statement. Moreover, as Paul Hersey (1984) points out, leaders' influence over the behavior of others is granted by the followers. Leaders can do nothing to force commitment to a vision. Rather, it must be something that speaks to the aspirations deep within each individual. Such a shared vision inspires and unleashes people's energies. It gives them an exciting purpose. Without it, work is just something to do to finance people's weekends. Workers get bogged down in administrative detail and the meaningless politics of their own personal squabbling. Such an atmosphere is the enemy of growth. It dooms an organization to mediocrity. As Peter Senge (1990, p. 209) says, "Without a pull toward some goal which people truly want to achieve, the forces in support of the status quo can be overwhelming. . . . In the absence of a great dream, pettiness prevails."

Chapter Five

Creating an Effective Organizational System

Effective leaders create an effective system for getting things done. They know that inefficient systems destroy commitment, pride, and self-esteem. All too often, the system they inherit takes a toll on worker motivation and makes legendary performance impossible. Managers seldom see that a system is a source of poor performance, however. When things aren't going well, they tend to blame the people rather than the established system of doing things. Confronted with the symptoms of an inefficient system—poor communication, low morale, and long delays in getting things done—they attack these symptoms piecemeal. They contract for training in communications skills, encourage supervisors to give more recognition, conduct time-and-motion studies, or establish the position of "expediter." They bring in dynamic speakers to pump up their people, to convince them that they are winners.

Such attempts help in the same way that treating the symptoms of a disease helps treat the disease. You might, for example, complain to your doctor about your headache, upset stomach, and inability to sleep because of a fever and coughing fits. If she prescribes aspirin, Pepto-Bismol, a sleeping pill, and cough syrup, she may improve the way you feel, but you still might die of pneumonia. Similarly, many new leaders learn of the symptoms of poor organization but fail to diagnose the disease. In a sense, the problem is masked by the symptoms. The capacity to look beyond them and see that the problem is rooted in the system is a critical leadership ability. In his landmark book, *The Fifth Discipline*, Peter Senge notes that we often think of the leader as the captain of the ship, determining the heading and giving the orders to those less capable. "The neglected role of leadership is the *designer* of the ship. . . . It is fruitless to be the leader in an organization that is poorly designed" (1990, p. 341).

One United Way chapter in a large city recently spent thousands of dollars on a training program to improve the self-image of its employees. The program has been used in many organizations and is highly effective. After participating in the program, these employees became more confident and saw more possibilities for themselves. They no longer accepted the limits of their old beliefs. They developed an eye for opportunities and a skill called possibility thinking. In short, they developed a winning attitude. Once they completed their training, several of them looked at the inflexible, bureaucratic structure in which they worked and saw little there for them to win, however. As a result of their new attitude, they were no longer willing to accept the limitations of such a system and left the agency for more hospitable work environments.

The System as Enemy

Sometimes ways of doing things evolve in such a manner that they seem to have a life of their own. No one seems to be responsible for the inefficiencies of the system. For example, as the new mayor of a medium-size city, Sensenbrenner (1991) learned upon assuming office that it took nine days, on average, to get a vehicle repaired in the city garage. In such a situation, it is tempting to jump to the conclusion that the people working in the garage are lazy or inept or that managers are allowing workers to waste time. In this case, however, the mayor decided to investigate the situation more thoroughly.

He visited the garage, a place no mayor had ever gone before, and asked how repairs could possibly take so long, when he could take his own car to a dealer and get it repaired the same day. The people in the garage agreed that repairs took too long but blamed the problem on the parts department, which seldom had the parts they needed in stock. The mayor then visited the parts manager, who in turn blamed the problem on the purchasing department, which bought so many different models of equipment every year that it was financially prohibitive to stock all the parts for each model. The mayor then visited the purchasing manager, who in turn blamed the comptroller of the city for requiring him to purchase whatever vehicle cost the least at buying time. The mayor informed the comptroller that this policy was costing the city dearly in equipment downtime. The comptroller agreed that it was a shortsighted policy but blamed the city attorney for the system. Exasperated, the mayor demanded that the city attorney tell him why equipment could not be purchased in a more rational way. The city attorney was baffled by this question, asserting that the city did not have to purchase the cheapest models at all.

In such a system, people feel helpless to control their lives, and as pointed out in Chapter Three, people feel depressed when they feel helpless. A task of leadership is to create a system that unleashes people's positive attitudes by enabling them to control the factors that affect their work. When leaders fail to pay attention to the demotivating effects of a system, their organization suffers. A 1990 national survey in Great Britain found that 80 percent of volunteers who quit said they would have continued volunteering if the agency they worked for were better organized and could have used them more effectively. As Karl Albrecht (1990, p. 54) wrote, "Too many organizations are at war with themselves as a result of the way they have organized and deployed resources and the way they have divided up responsibilities." It is difficult to gain commitment to the organization's purpose when the organization is at war with itself.

Fragmenting Responsibility

In seminars for government managers, I sometimes demonstrate how systems fragment responsibility by asking participants to create a system for mailing a letter that contains the inefficiencies that they struggle with each day. Following is one example of the kind of system they create.

- There would be a separate unit of the department to handle all mailing. Anyone who wanted a letter mailed would have to take it to that unit.

- One person would be responsible for receiving letters from the department employees who wanted them mailed. He or she would log in each letter and give the customer a receipt, keeping a copy of the receipt for the unit.

- A clerk would make two copies of each letter received by the unit, one for the files and one for the originator of the letter.

- The original letter would go to a section that would record the name of the intended recipient in a log book.

- The letter would then go to a letter review section. There, one employee would proofread it, another would review it for offensive content, a third would make sure the facts in the letter were accurate, and a fourth would check the letter for its adherence to department format standards. If any problems were found in any of these four areas, the letter would be returned to the originator, who would correct the defects and initiate the process all over again.

- Once the letter was approved by the review section, it would go to an address verification section, where someone would check the address to make sure it was accurate.

- The letter would then go to the folding section, where a supervisor would decide how many folds the letter required. A different person would then make each fold.

- The letter would next be sent to the envelope section, where a person would type the address on an envelope.

- The letter and accompanying envelope would then go to a stuffing section, where the letter would be placed in the envelope.

- The letter would then be sent to a quality control section, where a supervisor would oversee the completion of the following tasks: removing the letter from the envelope, checking to make sure the folds were straight, checking to make sure the address on the envelope matched the address on the letter, and restuffing the envelope. Each of these operations would be performed by a different person. If any problems were found, the quality control supervisor would write a variance report, and the letter would be returned to the unit where the error had been made and someone in that unit would make the required correction.

- Once a letter and envelope were approved by the quality control section, they would go to a weighing section, where a section employee would determine the amount of postage required.

- The letter and envelope would then be sent to the stamping section, where one employee would lick and affix the approved stamps on the envelope. Another employee would note how many of what kind of stamps were used and send this information to the stamp purchasing department.

- The letter and envelope would then go to a second quality control section, which would make sure the postage was accurate.

- The letter and envelope would next be sent to a sealing section where the envelope would be sealed.

- Each sealed envelope would be checked against the original log to make sure that no letters were lost in the process.

- The sealed envelope would be sent to a section where "RUSH" would be stamped on it.

- The letter in its sealed envelope would then be sent to the delivery section, where it would be trucked to the post office.

- At each step in the process, personnel would fill out a tracking form so that the status of each letter could be traced each day. Managers would take these forms home at night to keep up with the progress of each letter, look for bottlenecks, and add additional people to overcome snags in the system.

This inventive system would, of course, require a huge support network, a stamp purchasing department, a motor pool, a finance section, and so on. There might also be regional offices that would duplicate many of these functions. Furthermore, we could imagine organizing the system into divisions, with an operations division to do the actual folding, stuffing, and sealing; a quality control division to check the work of the operations unit; a planning division that would include committees to make sure, for example, that the organization did not buy stamps that would be regarded as offensive by any member of the public; a records division; and a support services division to handle such matters as personnel, training, and fiscal control. The managers of these divisions would report to various deputy directors, who would in turn report to an executive director of the entire system. All decisions would be months in coming because of the many parties involved.

Although people find this example amusing, it is also painfully similar to how modern organizations are run. It is what Leonard Schlesinger and James Heskett (1991) call "an industrial model." In service organizations, including governmental and nonprofit agencies, it is a prescription for difficulty. As Schlesinger and Heskett point out, such a system "sets in motion a cycle of failure that is uniformly bad for customers, employees, . . . and the country. Among its symptoms are customer disaffection, high employee turnover, . . . and little or no growth in productivity" (p. 71).

The main feature of such a system is to fragment responsibility by making each job require the least skill necessary. Jobs requiring several skills are replaced with jobs requiring only one skill. Logically, this should make it easier to find people who can do the jobs and easier to train them to succeed at the jobs. Furthermore, as an individual does the operation over and over at work each day, he should get better and better at it. The problem with this approach, overlooked by most managers, is that it makes legendary performance impossible. As Patricia O'Toole (1991, p. 22) notes, "What ever sense deskilling might make in the abstract, workers hate it. Routine . . . work—typing insurance-claim numbers all day long, for example—has always been spiritual novocaine."

Once such a system is set up, however, it is easy to justify the continuation of each function. People in such an enterprise often see no alternative way of doing things and suffer a system that drains the joy of life from the worker and makes commitment impossible. If, for example, someone were to suggest that the writers of the letters in our previous example could be trusted to write them well, that the letters did not have to be reviewed for form and content, many people would scoff. "Oh sure, just send any old thing out. Why care about our professional image?" They could also undoubtedly point to examples of inaccurate, unprofessional, or tactless letters that had been corrected because of the system. Similarly, if one challenged the need to check to make sure the postage was accurate, people would have stories about times when it wasn't. "We can't just let people put any amount they feel like on an envelope." Such justifications make the structure seem reasonable. It starts to sound like the only way to do things. The fact that the structure saps commitment is regarded as a necessary evil. Or the lack of commitment is blamed on the poor quality of the employees' work or on the ineffectiveness of the managers. But all the management training or personal effectiveness seminars in the world won't improve the commitment and performance of the employees, because the problem is inherent in the system.

Many would-be leaders are undone by the creative rationalizations of their bureaucrats. Sharon Pratt Dixon, for example, was elected mayor of Washington, D.C. in part because of her pledge to cut two thousand middle-management positions from the city's bloated bureaucracy. This should have been easy to do. Washington has one city employee for every eleven residents, a figure that is 80 percent higher than the national average of combined state and local governments. However, as reported in the *Economist,* her staff drew up "ingenious arguments to show the indispensability of their posts," with the result that the size of government increased by one thousand employees during her first nine months in office ("Washington's Mayor," 1991, p. 30).

The fragmentation of responsibility was originally designed in the industrial world to make manufacturing more efficient. In the world of providing services, however, fragmented responsibility is always inefficient. For example, one insurance company "estimated that it took an average of 22 days to approve a policy—during which time the papers were worked on for a mere 17 minutes. The rest of the time was spent shuffling papers between specialists; from credit-checkers to actuaries to salespeople and back" ("Reinventing Companies," 1991, p. 67). At the University of Michigan Hospitals in 1987, it took more than two hours to admit a patient. When one person was put in charge of the whole process, the admission time dropped to an average of eleven minutes (Siler and Garland, 1991, p. 112). In government and nonprofit organizations, the slowness of fragmented systems in getting things accomplished sometimes seems inevitable. People get trapped in what writer Andrew Smith once called "the willful procrastination of endless procedure." The purpose of the organization gets blurred in the process of getting through the day.

In the nonprofit world, hospitals typically suffer the most from a fragmented organizational structure. Thomas F. Hanrahan (1991, p. 33) describes this as a "structural complexity trap that saps human energy and often paralyzes the organization." It also leads to higher costs of doing business in an age when all nonprofits are in a fierce battle for resources. According to J. Philip Lathrop, vice president of health care practice at Booz-Allen & Hamilton (as reported by Weber, 1991, p. 24), "For every dollar spent on direct care, we spend $3 to $4 waiting for it to happen, arranging to do it, and writing it down." The traditional approach to such a problem is to do the steps faster, but Lathrop points out that in a fragmented system, speed doesn't solve the problem. "Once you've decided you're going to have centralized phlebotomy . . . it doesn't matter how fast the poor phlebotomist runs from room to room."

One of the skills of true leaders is to determine whether the system itself is the problem. If it is, leaders in today's world must cut through the rationalizations and excuses and excise the extra steps and functions that make things take longer and cost more. In doing so, they free their people from a system that destroys commitment and, ultimately, service.

Destroying Commitment

A system of getting work done can inadvertently destroy commitment in three ways. First, as in the letter-mailing example, it can fragment responsibility for a whole product among as many people as possible. This drains the life out of an enterprise and removes any possibility of pride. The more handoffs there are in the chain of events that produce a product, the more diluted a person's sense of ownership will be. Without ownership, there is no possibility of pride in one's work.

For example, in a state highway department, an engineer designs a bridge. He gives his notes on the design concept to another person, who uses computer-aided design and drafting software to create a drawing of the bridge. Someone else then figures out the specifications that should be placed in a contract to build the bridge. Another person writes a request for proposals and still another person approves it. Others review the proposals from contractors. Another person approves the awarding of the contract. The contractor builds the bridge, and someone else monitors the contractor. Another person does a final inspection. All of these people work in different units of the highway department. All of them tend to make minor modifications in the original design concept. As a consequence, nobody in the department gets much sense of pride in the quality of the bridge that is finally put into service.

Recently, I was told about what had once been a commitment-producing system in an accounting unit of a government agency. The unit had been organized in such a way that each person was responsible for a fund. One worker, for example, was responsible for all activities relating to accounting for the capital project fund. Another was responsible for all functions related to the revolving fund. Similarly, others were responsible for all activities related to other types of funds. The unit had real esprit de corps. People looked forward to going to work and got a great deal of satisfaction from being in charge of an entire fund. They felt important and valuable. Then a new manager took over and reorganized things so that instead of being responsible for a fund, each person was responsible for one function in all funds. For example, one person was put in charge of accounts receivable for all the funds. Another was assigned accounts payable, another was responsible for collection, and so on. Work became very boring; people started to dread it. They no longer had a sense of pride. The manager complained about his people's lack of commitment, believing that their "bad attitude" reflected something inherently wrong in them, not realizing that such an attitude is the inevitable result of fragmenting responsibility for a whole product.

Fragmentation produces conflict, duplication of effort, frustration, and a waste of energy in gaining approval and in coordinating efforts, and it destroys commitment. It leads to endless meetings to coordinate the fragmented efforts of people who are cut off from the end product of their efforts and leads to the creation of new and otherwise unnecessary jobs to expedite the fragmented process.

The second way that an organization system can destroy commitment is by communicating the idea that the workers cannot be trusted to do a good job. Quality control units or checkers are hired to find errors in the work. This produces low-level resentment and also leads to an apathetic view of the work. After all, if I make a mistake, the quality control person will see to it that it gets corrected. And if she doesn't, it will be her fault, not mine, that the mistake got through.

This commonly happens when upper layers of management decide to review and redo the work of the people below them. In one utility, a customer service representative complained that her letters to customers were rewritten by ten layers of management above her, with succeeding layers changing the changes. This destroyed her commitment to do her best ("It'll just be changed anyway") and took up to two weeks for customers to get a response. In a small department of state government, people in outlying offices who used to send their work directly to citizens now have to fax it to headquarters for review and revision. One employee was incensed when his boss, in such a review, told him that *mindful* was not a real word. ("What are you trying to say?" asked the angry note. "Don't make words up!") Effective leaders have little patience with such energy-draining and commitment-destroying activities. They hire top managers to lead, not to act as assistant proofreaders to first-line employees.

A third way in which the system can destroy commitment is by not giving people the authority to make decisions. This, in turn, makes it impossible for workers to take initiative. A state highways crew, for example, goes to work each morning having no idea what they will be doing that day. They arrive to find their daily tasks written on a white board, having been decided upon by management earlier the same morning. While in the middle of doing one task, they may be told to drop it and to do something else that management has suddenly decided has a higher priority. Such a system increases crew members' stress, fuels their antagonism, and finally creates apathy and alienation.

In one state agency, frontline supervisors must take the following eight steps to hire someone:

1. Request approval to fill the vacancy from the associate director (the immediate supervisor).
2. If approved, request a register of five top applicants plus top three minority applicants from personnel.
3. Interview all eight candidates.
4. Recommend a candidate to the associate director, who then interviews the candidate.
5. If the associate director approves of the candidate, write a memo describing the strengths and weaknesses of all eight candidates and why the one is being recommended.
6. Send the memo, along with the applications and test scores, through the associate director to the deputy director of the agency.
7. If the deputy director approves, forward the memo to the director of the agency.
8. If the director approves, offer the elected candidate the position.

Although some of these steps may seem to be pro forma, in practice supervisors have had their recommendations turned down by the associate director, the deputy director, and even the director of the agency, the latter two of which had never met the people involved. This has produced immense frustration in the first-line supervisors, who lack the authority to hire the person they feel is best qualified to do a job. It also makes for a long hiring authorization process, during which time a preferred applicant has sometimes accepted a job elsewhere.

Such a system, in which people in leadership positions are immersed in the details of what goes on three levels below them in the hierarchy, makes first-line supervisors feel that they are not trusted and reduces their self-confidence and self-esteem. Moreover, it gets in the way of their doing their work to the best of their abilities. It is impossible to be committed to a purpose in such frustrating circumstances.

These three aspects of a commitment-destroying system can be made worse by combining them with a management philosophy of keeping people in the dark about why they do what they do and of withholding recognition, thereby causing people to feel that their efforts not only have little meaning but are also unappreciated. As indicated in Chapter Two, such a philosophy significantly undercuts the leader's ability to influence.

Streamlining the Work Flow

A leader ensures that progress is made toward the realization of the mission by creating a system of organization that promotes movement. Tracking the work flow in the existing system allows the leader to begin the major task of cutting through the mass of handoffs, functions, and fragmentations that bogs down so many organizations.

Many inefficiencies may be masked by the way the work is structured. A state personnel department, for example, had a counter where a clerk directed job seekers to announcements of state job openings in their fields. If they found a job of interest, they would fill out an application. The remaining steps in the process were as follows:

1. The clerk would accept the application and inform the applicant that, if she was qualified, she would be notified within three weeks. The clerk also explained the process by which the applicant would be tested and interviewed.
2. The clerk would send the application to a person whose job was to determine if the applicant met the minimum qualifications for the job by comparing the requirements of the job with the information provided on the application form.
3. If the candidate was not qualified she would receive a form letter, which included a notice of her right to appeal the determination. If the candidate was qualified, the application would be sent to a clerk who entered the candidate's information into a computer file. This file became a register from which a manager could select candidates to be interviewed.

In this situation, managers complained about how long it took to build a register, and applicants complained about how long it took to get hired. In the past, managers in the personnel department had tried to hurry things along by exhorting the people responsible for the three-step process to work more efficiently.

The system itself, however, was inefficient. At each step in the process, the application had to wait until the next person got to it. An alternative to this system would be to have each of the three people do all three steps. That is, each employee could receive applications, compare the information given with the minimum job requirements while applicants were still present, tell applicants if they were or were not qualified and get additional information if necessary (thus avoiding costly appeals), and enter the data into the computer to build the register.

All of this could happen in a matter of minutes rather than weeks. Such a system could also give workers a better connection to the customer and a greater sense of responsibility for doing a good job. In large organizations, leaders can find thousands of such small opportunities for improving the system.

Before such a system can be implemented, of course, the three workers need to be trained to do the steps with which they are unfamiliar. During this training period, the organization will experience a drop in productivity. This drop is more than offset in the long run by the increased efficiency of having all steps completed by one person, but it can give ammunition to the leader's critics. Leaders must have the courage to persist in these early stages and to encourage people to have faith in the process.

Changing such a system in government is fraught with obstacles. There were three separate job classifications for the three steps. To combine them, a new classification had to be created. Such obstacles do not stop leaders. They persist with a passion to create a better situation.

To improve your own system, look for places where the work changes hands and see if the steps can be combined, as in the above example. Also look for conflicts around "turf" issues. A western museum, for example, spent months arguing over the definition of donor and member. The development office wanted the amount of money that would make a person a donor set low, so they would get credit for having a donor. The membership office wanted it set high, so they would get credit for another member. Leaders see that such arguments are a waste of energy. One way to avoid them is to combine the two units into one.

Giving People Ownership

The first step in developing a system that encourages excellence is to make sure that each worker has "ownership." By this I mean that the employee or volunteer has something of his or her own to be responsible for—clients, geographical area, event, or product. Ownership implies that the worker (or, in some cases, a team of workers) controls all that happens on his or her turf and that the worker alone is responsible for the success or failure of the activities conducted with relation to that turf. It gives the person or team the ability to say, "This is mine." For volunteers and staff in the nonprofit world, the turf is most often a client or project. There are many examples of volunteers who have such responsibility. Big brothers, phone workers in a crisis clinic, senior companions, and foster grandparents are all volunteers who have one or more clients who are "theirs."

When jobs are transformed in this way, workers report an increase in pride in their work and in job satisfaction, and management finds that errors, absenteeism, turnover, and grievances decline dramatically.

Yet this way of organizing work is in direct contradiction to the way work is normally organized. Traditional systems fragment responsibility. Ownership is absent when people do only one of many activities an agency conducts in providing a particular service to a particular person or group. In some social service agencies, for example, a receptionist takes information from potential clients and then hands the resulting paperwork over to someone else to determine their eligibility for services. When people merely do one activity in a string of activities that finally ends up in a client's being served, they lose the intense satisfaction of helping others that produces commitment. Although they know that somewhere down the line they have contributed to the client's being served, their sense of pride is diluted by all the others who have had a hand in doing this. Similarly, volunteers fixing up a school will tend to get more satisfaction if they do all the activities related to fixing up a particular room than if they do one activity (such as painting or washing windows) in all the rooms. The first circumstance provides them with a sense of ownership ("this is my room"). In the second case, however, feelings of ownership and responsibility are missing or diluted; because the volunteers' sense of pride in the work is reduced, they tend to burn out much faster than those who have full responsibility for a client or project.

An example of team ownership comes from an all-volunteer program that was formed when a parks department reduced maintenance personnel during a budget cut. Teams of volunteers were assigned parks of their own, which they kept free of trash and graffiti. In this case, the sense of ownership was met because a team could look at "their" park and take pride in its appearance.

The difference between a team and a collection of isolated individuals who lack ownership is that a team has the authority to plan and evaluate its work and agree on who is going to do what. At a large airport, for example, teams of janitors are each assigned a concourse. Every night, members of the team decide what cleaning is necessary, who will do what, when to stop, and when to take breaks. In a fragmented system, someone else makes those decisions. If people have any say at all in what they are to do, it is limited to the small, isolated activities for which they are responsible.

While the traditional approach, based more on manufacturing than on providing services, may once have worked better than it does now, today's managers will always suffer from undermotivated workers when work is fragmented in the standard way. Today's workers simply do not look forward to spending a whole day doing a repetitive job that a monkey could do. They do so only because they have to make a living. Their work life is thus an unpleasant necessity, a drab expanse between weekends. They invest little thought or creative energy in their work because neither is called for. Without a sense of ownership, they contribute only a fraction of their potential worth to the organization.

Effective organizations find it easier to get results, in part, because their workers want to do the work. They look forward to work each day because it satisfies them. And such workers will always produce better results than those who work only to earn a living. The property management division of a large electric utility

provides an example of how motivation increases and workers become more effective when leaders give them some ownership. Before
the workers in this division were given ownership, the office was
divided into three sections. The acquisition section was responsible
for acquiring property and easements for power lines and substa-
tions. The management section was responsible for renting property, removing encroachments, and granting easements to others.
The disposition section was responsible for selling surplus proper-
ties and releasing easements. As is common in many organizations,
each unit was restricted to performing one repetitive function. Six
agents worked in the division, two in each unit. Because they got
bored performing the same function over and over, they were occasionally transferred to other units. Nonetheless, they experienced
very little job satisfaction.

To create ownership for each agent, the leader divided the
utility's service region into six geographic areas and assigned one
agent to handle all functions (relating to acquisition, management,
and disposition) for all property within an area. New employees of
the division serve an apprenticeship period with the division supervisor, getting training and close supervision until they have developed enough expertise to handle all functions on their own. As is
always the case, the employees now describe themselves as satisfied,
highly motivated, and hardworking. Having ownership, they feel
more important.

Giving people ownership not only motivates them, but it
enables the leader to get away from the details of each employee's
work. In the foregoing example, before the workers had ownership,
the supervisor had to assign every issue regarding property management to the appropriate section. After each agent was given ownership, the supervisor no longer had to contend with assessing and
assigning such issues. As a consequence, he had the opportunity to
consider more strategic matters, such as creating a vision of a better
world for the organization. It is impossible to lead unless your eyes
are focused on the horizon, and this is impossible if you are looking
down at the details of the work going on below you.

Traditional managers often resist the idea of giving a worker
ownership, perhaps because it is such a radical change; most would
like to get better results without doing anything very different. In

response to the stress these managers feel when forced to consider such a change, many of them grope for excuses as to why they can't make the change: "the union wouldn't stand for it"; "my boss wouldn't go for this." For those who find the initial strength to act, to give their workers ownership, however, life becomes far less stressful. It is much easier to succeed in any endeavor when people you lead share your sense of ownership and pride in the enterprise.

Promoting Efficiency

In addition to being the enemies of the status quo, leaders are also the relentless enemies of wasted, bureaucratic effort. Inefficient systems inflate the cost of doing things. If the system is accepted as is, the cost seems inescapable. In one county public works department, for example, a manager was responsible for scheduling work in response to complaints from the public. He scheduled this work in the order in which the complaints were received, with the most recent complaint last on the list. At one point there was a backlog of about two months' worth of complaints.

A new director of the department examined the scheduling of work and noted that it resulted in a lot of moving of equipment. The machine to unclog blocked culverts, for example might be in the northwest part of the county in the morning, moved to the southeast part of the county to unblock another culvert in the afternoon, then moved back to the northwest the next day to clean out a third culvert. He instructed the scheduling manager to change his system, to give the work crew a list of all blocked culverts and ask them to schedule them according to proximity rather than order of complaint. As a result, much less time was wasted in moving equipment and more time was spent cleaning out culverts. By taking this approach, the department managed to work through its backlog of complaints. Productivity rose, resulting in more service to citizens at less cost per unit of service.

In a Florida hospital, two-person teams made up of a nurse and a technician each "own" four to seven patients. They do almost everything for them, including "records processing . . . admitting, charting, tray passing, transportation . . . room clean-up, care planning, assessment, therapeutic intervention, diagnostic test administration, and outcome evaluation" (Weber, 1991, p. 25). Although it may seem inefficient to have a highly skilled person doing something like picking up trays, the experiment produced enormous gains in quality of care and hospital morale, and a dramatic reduction in costs.

When leaders change systems to make them more efficient, there is often some resistance from those who are used to the old way of doing things. They often hear "We can't do that" or "It won't work that way," or "You don't understand." The best means of countering this is to involve the resisters in defining a better method. Alternately, leaders can always fall back on authority. When Larry Combs became general manager at a Parker-Hannifin plant and encountered resisters who exclaimed, "We can't do that," he replied, "Yes we can; I'm the boss."

Leaders' natural enmity toward wasting time and energy is allied with their focus on change. Leaders don't get trapped by the status quo because they are always thinking about how to make things better in the future. People who focus instead on the present and the past tend not to spot inefficiencies because they have always done things one way. For example, each year employees in all of one state's agencies fill out a form describing their job duties. The forms are given to each agency's personnel officer, who reviews them and then sends them on to the state personnel department, where an analyst makes sure that the duties match the job class assigned to each individual. In more than 95 percent of the cases, they do match. These forms, from all the agencies, are stacked in profusion on analysts' desktops. No one has questioned why the analysts review the forms for everyone instead of just reviewing the ones that the agency personnel officers regard as problems. The system has always been this way, wasting the time and the life of the analysts. Such a situation cries out for leadership, for someone with the vision and courage to free people from such inefficiency.

Being purpose-oriented individuals, leaders free their people from the mass of meaningless activity that consumes too much energy in today's government and nonprofit organizations. As Peter Drucker (1991, p. 72) says, "The first questions in increasing productivity [in service work] have to be, 'What is the task? What are we trying to accomplish? Why do it at all?'" The last question is the most critical for leaders who seek to liberate their people from the shackles of low-payoff activities and to direct their energies to something worthwhile.

In this time of scarce resources, effective leaders are concerned that their people work in a lean organization. Jobs such as quality control specialist, expediter, and vice president for planning are eliminated by effective leaders. The activities these people perform in traditional organizations, usually at the management level, are either eliminated or are done by the workers themselves. The result is a more efficient organization with lower overhead.

By giving people ownership, leaders also increase efficiency by reducing the need for meetings and other management efforts at coordination. Traditional organizations split responsibility for results and must then spend great amounts of time and effort reassembling what they have rent asunder—coordinating fragmented efforts, clarifying ownership, and dealing with the political battles that inevitably arise when people find that the impact of their work can be altered by the performance and values of others who have a hand in the final outcome.

By giving people the responsibility of ownership, leaders avoid these fragmentation problems and also lay the foundation for streamlining their organizations. Essentially, streamlining means creating efficiency, getting the same amount of work done with fewer administrators and managers. As the previous examples show, this can be done even in small organizations. More will be said about streamlining in Chapter Seven.

Relating the System to the Mission

In creating the system, the leader translates the strategic goals of the organization into a series of results to be achieved by individuals or teams, thereby helping people see that their efforts are connected to the realization of the mission. These results are arranged in a logical hierarchy so that the achievement of the lower ones automatically leads to the achievement of higher goals.

The hierarchy of the organization should follow this logical hierarchy of results. For example, a water quality specialist in the Washington State Department of Ecology might have a goal of

reducing toxic emissions from a sewage treatment plant on the Duwamish River. His boss might have the larger goal of making the
Duwamish River safe for humans and fish. The achievement of the
specialist's goal would contribute directly to the achievement of
the supervisor's goal. This would continue up the hierarchy of the
organization, with successive levels having goals related to the water
quality of Puget Sound, into which the Duwamish flows, the water
quality of western Washington, and the water quality of Washington State. The achievement of the goal of safe water in all of Washington State would in turn contribute to the department's mission
of ensuring a safe and pleasant environment for the citizens of the
state.

This, in fact, is not the way this organization is structured.
Water quality programs are divided according to the functions of
giving grants to others and of taking direct action. The resulting
two units sometimes inadvertently wind up working at cross-
purposes or duplicating each other's efforts, not because of poor
management but because of the inevitable consequence of the
structure.

Such a structure can be frustrating for a leader. Some managers use the structure as an excuse for not doing things or for the
ineffectiveness of their units. Leaders work to create a structure that
enables people to unleash their energy toward accomplishing the
organization's mission. By creating a logical hierarchy of goals,
leaders "align" the efforts of all people in the organization toward
a common purpose. As Senge (1990) points out, such an alignment
of purpose is necessary before we set about freeing people from
bureaucratic constraints. In order for people to use their increased
authority effectively, we must be sure that they do not work at cross-
purposes. According to Senge (p. 235), "Empowering the individual
when there is a relatively low level of alignment worsens the chaos
and makes managing the team even more difficult."

The building blocks of an effective organization are the individual jobs to be done. The principles that guide the leader in
designing motivating jobs are explored in the next chapter.

Chapter Six

Designing
Empowering Jobs

Earlier I said that effective leaders create a situation in which committed, self-confident people work in exciting jobs. We can see how seldom managers truly lead in this way by noting how many people regard their jobs as an odious interlude between weekends. In one of my seminars, I ask people for a definition of success. A depressing number define it as not having to go to work. Too many people waste their potential sitting at their desks counting the hours until quitting time, the days till the weekend, the weeks until the next holiday, the months till the next vacation.

Leaders can save these people from living their lives in this way by creating jobs they can look forward to, jobs that are interesting, challenging, and rewarding. By doing this, leaders not only enrich the work lives of their people but unleash a tremendous amount of motivational energy to get things done. This is important for all personnel, but it is particularly critical for volunteers. If leaders fail to give their volunteers jobs they want to do, turnover, unreliability, and low morale will result. A job people want to do is the cornerstone of all successful volunteer programs. While paid employees will do a job that they find emotionally unrewarding because they are monetarily compensated for doing so, volunteers will not do so for long. This has given volunteers in general a reputation of being unreliable. On the contrary, if the volunteer does not find the job to be personally satisfying, he or she can be relied upon to quit.

Nonprofit and public sector programs are successful when volunteers and staff members have jobs they look forward to and want to do. In Chapter Five we saw how leaders create a work system that makes the work more rewarding. In this chapter, we look at the way leaders can design individual jobs so that people want to do them.

The Motivating Power of Games

The people who show up for work that has been designed according to standard management principles often do so not out of a love for the work but out of a desire to earn a salary. When we detect low interest, we tend to think that something is lacking in the workers. However, most people are not intrinsically unmotivated. They usually do look forward to something in their lives. It is just that the design of their work does not provide them with the same motivation.

Imagine that we are at the finals of the Olympic track competition. Down on the green infield of the stadium, the finest runners in the world are assembled. For the past four years, these athletes have undergone a grueling training regimen, pushing themselves beyond their limits in the hope of getting to this day, when we and they will find out who the best runners in the entire world are. The runners are nervous and trying to psych themselves up, visualizing success, hoping to do the best they've ever done. The stadium is packed with fans from many countries (and the various steroid manufacturers), eager to cheer their various champions on to victory. Perhaps today they will see a truly legendary performance. The excitement is electric as the starter comes onto the track. "Okay," he says, "it's time to run."

One of the runners approaches the starter. "Excuse me," he says, "but I haven't seen a schedule. What event is this?"

"What do you mean?" replies the starter.

"Well, is this the 100 meters or the 1,500 meters or the marathon? What event is this?"

The starter looks confused. "Well, it isn't any particular event. It's just time to run."

"Well, where's the finish line?" asks the runner.

"There isn't any finish line," the starter responds in exasperation. "Now look. All these people paid good money and came thousands of miles to see you run. Get over there and show them how you do it."

Obviously, under such circumstances, the amount of effort the runners would put out would not be their maximum. The likelihood of legendary performance would be nil. They would quickly get bored and frustrated and wander off the field.

I have told you this tale because a great many people at work today are like runners with no finish lines. They have much to do, but it is just running, just something to do. Designed this way, their jobs have little meaning or interest. Like the runners, they become bored and frustrated and mentally wander off the field. In such circumstances, managers tend to complain about the low quality of the people they supervise. Leaders realize that the system and the design of the job are the problem.

I also told you this story to indicate that designers of games have always been much better than designers of work at creating human activities that people want to perform. Those who design jobs for salaried and volunteer staff members might, therefore, more productively follow the principles of those who design games.

Games are voluntary activities that are designed to be intrinsically motivating. Many games are so motivating that people will spend a great deal of time and money on expensive equipment and lessons in order to get better at them, a thing that is rarely true of work. Some games are so well designed, in fact, that people will spend lots of money just to see other people play them.

The Elements of Well-Designed Jobs

The point I want to make here is not that work should be a game but that jobs should have the same motivational elements that games do. All games have four characteristics that jobs can also have but seldom do. One of these elements, ownership, was discussed at length in Chapter Five. The other three elements of a well-designed job—responsibility, authority, and accountability—are described in the rest of this section. (See also Lynch, 1988.)

Responsibility for Results

A manager's job, you may have heard it said, is to achieve planned results through other people. This simple statement has many implications. One is that those other people are responsible for achieving results and therefore should know what those results are supposed to be. Most workers feel no such responsibility, however. Their jobs are not designed to give it to them.

Most jobs are not defined in terms of results or outcomes. Instead, a typical job description merely lists a series of activities that a person is supposed to perform. The result is never mentioned. In fact, the responsibility for the result is usually fragmented; several people, who each perform a few activities, contribute to the result. Indeed, responsibility is sometimes so fragmented that the worker, paid or volunteer, loses sight of the result. As a direct consequence of this, results are poorly and inefficiently obtained, and those performing the activities get bored. Consultant John Carver (1990, p. 56) states, "The only justifiable reason for organizational existence is the production of worthwhile results." When leaders do not define results, people lose connection to that purpose, and commitment suffers.

Emphasis is placed on activities when leaders focus their attention on what goes on inside the unit of the organization they lead. As Peter Drucker (1988, p. 76) notes, however, "The single most important thing to remember about any enterprise is that there are no results inside its walls . . . The result of a hospital is a healed patient. The result of a school is a student who has learned something."

Leaders of nonprofit and especially government organizations sometimes adopt this internal focus by concentrating on the amount of money they have to spend and the process they go through to spend it. In doing so, they lose sight of the results.

Political leaders trumpet how much money government has spent on a problem, but they rarely talk about the results of the activities that the money supported, perhaps because positive results are embarrassingly few.

To be effective, leaders must focus people on the outcome of their efforts. This emphasis can start with how the funding source (legislature or charitable group) regards the agency. As David Osborne (1990, p. 22) says, "Bureaucratic governments fund according to inputs: how many full-time positions are allotted, how many students enroll, how many people are poor enough to qualify. . . . When institutions are funded according to inputs they have little reason to strive for better performance. But when they are funded according to outcomes, they become obsessive about performance." Although few funding sources pay much attention to outcomes, the leaders of an organization must see that their people do. In this way they provide workers with a challenge, a sense of responsibility, and a sense of power.

Examples of Results. Because people are not used to thinking about work in terms of results, they often find the concept difficult to grasp. Let's look at some examples. For instance, a receptionist may think of his job as a number of activities such as answering the phone, greeting visitors, and telling people where to go. To define the result we want from such activities, we must ask why we want these things done. What is it the receptionist should be trying to accomplish? We might come up with a statement of result such as "People coming to the office will view us as a competent, professional organization."

A training officer in state government might be required to conduct a certain number of training sessions per month. By defining the job in this way, we give the trainer an activity that requires no apparent skill; it is merely something for the trainer to get through. Why do we want the training? To increase the skills of our people? Then we must make the trainer responsible for that. Similarly, a forest worker who is told that two of his job duties are to "issue burn permits and to provide information on the dangers of forest fires" will find the job more challenging if it is described in terms of the desired result: to eliminate forest fires that result from escaped small burns.

A teacher's aide might be told that one of her duties is to work with children on reading skills. Anyone can fulfill this part of the job description without trying because no result has been specified. When we ask only that someone "work with" children, we are not creating any responsibility for helping children learn. There is no challenge in the job when it is defined in this way. Rephrased in terms of the result we are after—to bring students' reading ability up one-half grade level, for example—the job inspires responsibility.

A maintenance worker in a city transit facility might be responsible not just for doing preventive maintenance but for increasing the number of miles between remedial repairs. A cleaner at the same facility might be responsible for the result that drivers will be satisfied with the cleanliness of their coaches.

A hospital volunteer might be told that her job is to visit patients' rooms with the hospitality cart. However, this does not tell the volunteer the desired future consequence of the activity of pushing the cart around. The volunteer doesn't understand the point of doing this, unless she figures it out for herself, and so the work lacks meaning. Again, the question we need to ask is, What are we trying to accomplish here? To make a profit from selling the items on the cart? Then we must give the volunteer responsibility for that. Or are we trying to reduce patients' feelings of isolation, anxiety, and boredom by giving someone an excuse to visit them? In that case, we must give the volunteer responsibility for that, for making a direct contribution toward a vision of the hospital in which patients feel comfortable and cared about.

Similarly, one way of describing the job of a Girl Scout leader is to say that she is to provide educational and recreational activities for girls. If we were going to state the job in terms of results, we might say that it is to help girls grow up viewing themselves as competent and valuable people. By putting the result in the job description, we keep the scout leader focused on the desired outcome she is trying to achieve. In this case, the result is difficult to achieve with complete success. It is nonetheless the goal the leader should have in mind as she works with her girls. In fact, the job is interesting and rewarding precisely because it is so challenging. It is more rewarding to be engaged in helping girls grow up with a strong self-image than it is to be responsible only for various activities such as hiking and singing songs. Some leaders back away from defining the job this way because they fear it is too challenging. By doing so, however, the job not only becomes less rewarding for the volunteer but it does a disservice to the girls.

In a certain town there were two hospitals, each of which was half full and in danger of going out of business. The food at both hospitals had a terrible reputation. I met with the food service workers at one of these hospitals to design a job that was more challenging. I asked them, "What are you trying to accomplish in your job?" Answers to this question indicated that they were not trying to accomplish anything except to cook the food. "What is the point of cooking the food?" I asked. One person suggested that it was so patients would get adequate nutrition. But after some discussion, the workers rejected that as a result because the nutritionist who planned the menu had control over what was prepared. "How would you know if you had done a good job cooking?" I asked. At this point, someone said that he based that judgment on how much food came back uneaten. This led us to define the result as "patients will find their meals appetizing."

Although we couldn't expect anything like 100 percent perfect performance from these workers (they are constrained by the nutritionist in terms of what they can prepare, and their "customers" are sick), they should nevertheless be trying to achieve this result every time they prepare a meal. This makes the job more challenging because while nearly anyone can prepare food, to prepare food that people find appetizing is more difficult.

Changing the job description to include responsibility for a result started to turn the competitive tide in favor of this hospital. Word got around town that the food was better here than at the other hospital. Patients began asking their doctors if they could go to the hospital with the better food. People who worked near the hospital started eating lunch in the hospital cafeteria. And the director of food service actually started a successful catering business out of the hospital kitchen.

As these examples illustrate, there are two primary benefits to defining jobs in terms of results. The first is that it helps to meet people's need for a sense of achievement or accomplishment. It helps them feel valuable. The second benefit is that it helps programs operate more effectively. Imagine the increase in effectiveness if schoolteachers, for example, were paid on the basis of whether their students learned something instead of on the basis of their longevity in the job or number of graduate courses completed, or if police officers were responsible for reducing burglaries instead of patrolling the streets, or if those administering anti-poverty programs were responsible for getting people out of poverty instead of providing services to the poor. When people know what they are supposed to accomplish, they are more likely to accomplish it.

Consequences of Holding People Responsible for Activities. Holding people responsible for performing job activities is like holding runners responsible for running. There is no finish line, and the workers get bored. Managers ignore this boredom at great cost because bored people seek excitement. With nothing exciting in the job, they may turn their attention to other things. Sometimes they find that playing practical jokes, filing grievances, or taking job actions provides the excitement they desire.

The other side of the coin is that if workers are not responsible for the outcome of their efforts, the manager shoulders the responsibility for the result. It is very stressful to be responsible for the outcome of activities you do not perform. So while workers go home to rejoice that the working day is done, the manager goes home and worries about the quality of the workers' performance. Not only does this produce great stress, but it also leads the manager to meddle in the details of the work. Since he or she is responsible for the outcome of what the workers do, the manager tends to monitor them closely or even tell them what to do. It is difficult to lead, to think about the future and the mission of the organization when one's brain is busy running other people's bodies, when one is immersed in the details of the work that one's people do.

Focusing on processes rather than outcomes also tends to waste a lot of money. Today, many organizations are involved in very expensive "total quality management" programs. Most of these, in the words of Robert Schaffer and Harvey Thomson (1992,

p. 80), "have as much impact on operational and financial results as a ceremonial rain dance has on the weather." This is because the focus is on establishing new bureaucracies and procedures rather than on affecting the outcome. As noted in "The Cracks in Quality" (1992, p. 67), too many organizations "have concentrated all their efforts on improving their quality processes, and lost sight of the customer on the way."

The leader's ability to think in terms of results makes programs more effective because people can always perform the activities without accomplishing the desired result. I had a student a few years ago who at one time had been a police officer in a large city. In this particular city, all rookies were placed on the graveyard shift. After about four o'clock in the morning, even the most heinous felons were at home in bed, and there wasn't much action. One of the things the officers were supposed to do was to find burned-out street lights and note their light pole numbers on a form the officers were given for that purpose. I suppose the point of this, the result that was desired, was to keep the streets well-lighted so that pools of darkness didn't form where criminals could gather and plot mayhem on an unsuspecting public. All the officers were told, however, was that they were supposed to locate burned-out street lights. In fact, they were instructed to find a minimum of two burned-out lights on each shift.

During his third night on duty, the rookie stopped by the doughnut shop for a cup of coffee at about 5:00 A.M. An old-timer on the force was sitting at the counter, also on his break. He asked the rookie how things were going. "Well, okay, I guess," said the rookie. "Except that tonight I'm having a devil of a time finding any burned-out street lights. I found two the first night. I found three last night, and I wish I had saved one of those for tonight because I can't find a single one."

"Why on earth would you want to do that?" the older officer asked.

"Well, because we have that form to fill out. We have to find two each night."

The old-timer shook his head. "Kid, what time of day do they change the bulbs in those lights?"

"I don't know," the rookie replied. "Sometime during the day, I guess."

"Right," responded the veteran officer. "They can't tell if they're burned out or not, can they? Just write down a couple of pole numbers. That's what the rest of us do."

If you are interested in results, define them. You will tend to get what people feel responsible for. If you want well-lighted streets, make that the responsibility of the officer. If you want pole numbers, ask only for that.

All of this does not mean that leaders should not care about the activities. They need to make sure that the activities are legal, in keeping with the values of the organization, and likely to be effective. (The Iran-Contra affair was perhaps an example of what happens when a person's boss cares only about the results and not the activities.) It does mean, however, that people should be focused on the outcome of their efforts. They are deemed to do a good job if their activities produce a desired effect, not if they are merely performed.

Team Responsibility. Thus far in this discussion of responsibility for results, the emphasis has been on giving the individual responsibility for an end product. In some situations, however, this is neither possible nor desirable. When many different technical skills need to be brought together to produce a result or when it is physically impossible for one person to do all the tasks required, a team should be given the responsibility for the result.

Many organizations use the word *team* to describe collections of workers that are not really teams at all. I have heard a supervisor refer to members of a typing pool as "my team," for example, even though each typist did isolated work on tasks assigned by the supervisor. Such workers are not really a team because they never have to work together to achieve a result. They do not do what a team does. They do not confer about what they will do to try to achieve their results; they do not plan strategy; they do not work together as a cohesive, thinking whole. Instead, the supervisor sets the strategy, does the thinking, and coordinates the activities, the very things that would allow the individuals to become a team.

For example, the desired result of a crew of workers surveying land for the purpose of putting in a new road might be "Designers will be satisfied with the quality of the survey information." The desired result for a team of designers for that project might be "Contractors will be able to build a good road from the team's plans." By defining each team's purpose in terms of these results, each worker will succeed if the team succeeds. The workers will also have some authority, as a group, to plan how to accomplish the result.

The Authority to Think

The authority to think is the second key element of well-designed jobs, whether for individuals or teams. With this authority the individual or team not only does the work but plays some part in deciding how to do it.

When we think of leaders, we sometimes think of people who give orders. However, individuals who make the day-to-day decisions for their people cannot be effective leaders. A leader is not likely to be a person who tells everyone else what to do because this tends to engender resentment and dilute the leader's power. Moreover, a person who is so involved in the details of her people's work that she can make knowledgeable daily assignments is unlikely to have the time necessary to act proactively, to act as a leader.

Many managers have a built-in resistance to allowing people this authority. Standard management practice holds that the supervisor plans and directs the actions of the subordinates. Employees carry out whatever the supervisor thinks should be done. Indeed, when people first come on board, this may be the most comfortable and effective way to proceed. As people learn the job and figure out what is going on, however, the fact that they are only doing what someone else decides begins to sap their motivation and minimize their feelings of pride in what they accomplish. When employees don't have the authority to think, when they are controlled by another person, they feel powerless. They react with feelings of resentment, apathy, or both. As one government mechanic said to me recently, "My boss screams at me to order parts to get an engine back in service fast. So I order the parts in a way that takes two weeks for them to reach us. I'll be darned if I'm going to give someone who treats me that way what he wants." Is this an attitude problem on the part of the worker? No, it is a management problem. Leaders make sure that they create a climate in which employees and volunteers can feel effective by empowering them to make their own decisions within the context of measurable results.

This does not mean that leaders should abdicate their responsibility for ensuring good results from people. Obviously, organizations cannot afford to have everyone doing whatever he or she thinks best, without any guidance. Leaders make sure that all members of the group are working toward the achievement of a coordinated set of goals. They do this by involving all members in the planning process so that they feel a sense of authority over the "how" of their jobs.

In designing a job, leaders ask such questions as "How would a person who tells the volunteer and paid staff member what to do know what to tell them?" Leaders then include those thinking tasks in the job description, eliminating a schism between thinking and doing. In a sense, in doing this they give the worker back his brain.

When workers have the authority to think, they provide faster and better service to clients. When frontline workers have the authority to decide what to do, they can take immediate action to serve clients. In the city of Austin, for example, building inspectors are allowed to make on-site decisions on changes to approved plans. In contrast, in many other cities, contractors and architects must wait for a decision from higher authority, which slows down the construction process.

Accountability for Results

The third critical element in well-designed jobs is accountability. This means that leaders must decide how to determine, or measure, whether the desired results are being achieved. If managers do not do this, the statement of result will have little motivating value, and it will be impossible for both the staff member and the supervisor to know how well the staff member is doing the job.

For some reason, many managers of the standard school, for all their authoritarian, "hardheaded" demands, are very meek about measuring employee performance in a way that truly holds the employee accountable. Of course, when they give no one else responsibility for results, they themselves are the only ones accountable for the success or failure of the enterprise. This is also true of more nurturing, supportive managers. Many volunteer managers, for example, shy away from measuring volunteer performance, thinking that doing so would discourage the volunteer or cause so much stress as to lead the volunteer to leave the organization. As with so much in management, however, the opposite is closer to the truth. If people can't tell how well they are doing, if they don't know whether they are succeeding or failing, they tend to get bored or frustrated with the activity. To return to our track meet analogy, runners who are just running, whose speed is not being measured, will have little incentive to put out more effort. Where there is no measurement of results, there is also no incentive to try a different course of action because workers will not know whether their present course is succeeding.

Good leadership is about tapping the best instincts and motives of the people being led. Leaders grant their people accountability to allow them a sense of accomplishment, of winning. Staff members and volunteers cannot feel they are winning, however, unless someone is keeping score and unless they know what that score is. If a hospital volunteer, for example, is visiting patients with the goal of making them feel more comfortable and less fearful and lonely, it is important that he be given some feedback on how well he is achieving this desired result. Such feedback can come from a survey of patients, either during or after their hospital stay. If the survey shows that the volunteer is making little difference, this information will naturally encourage him to try something different in a quest for a more effective approach.

The power of measuring performance is illustrated by the experience of the revenue department in a western state. The leader of revenue collection organized the work of the department according to the principles described in Chapter Five. Each revenue officer was responsible for making sure a certain group of businesses paid their due to the state. Businesses that owed the state money were termed "delinquent accounts." The leader began to compile and feed back to his people the percentage of delinquent accounts each of them had. Every quarter, each revenue officer received a printout showing his or her percentage and the percentages of the other officers. This information was sent without comment; there was no exhortation to do better, simply the reporting of a score. The first quarter this was done, the percentage of delinquent accounts ranged from 6 to 9 percent. This may not sound like a lot, but it amounted to tens of millions of dollars. In the second quarter, the number dropped to between 5 and 7 percent. For the third quarter, between 4 and 6 percent of the accounts were delinquent, and in the fourth quarter, the figure dropped to between 3 and 5 percent. Fourth quarter tax revenues were over $15 million more than those of the first quarter. At this point, the leader felt that his people had reached their maximum potential, that this was about as good as they could do. Nevertheless, he kept sending out the percentages, and the numbers kept dropping (though not as dramatically).

Why the change? For the first time, people knew how they were doing in comparison to each other. They also, over time, were able to compare their current score with their previous personal best. This gave them an extra incentive to do even better. Without a score, there was little incentive to do anything differently than they had done before.

When things stay the same, never getting better, there is no movement. And where there is no movement, no leadership is being exercised. By making sure people get feedback on the effect of their actions, leaders make them accountable for those actions and encourage them to improve. By giving workers responsibility for a result and then measuring the degree to which they achieve it, leaders create a situation in which the worker's own ego and sense of self-worth are inextricably woven into the achievement of organizational objectives. By contrast, in organizations where traditional managers give workers no responsibility or accountability and confine them to a narrow set of activities, ego and sense of self-worth have no natural outlet on the job. Workers may therefore look for other ways of "winning," such as seeing how little of the spirit and intent of the supervisor's instructions they can carry out. A leader's most powerful resource can be that workers' egos are working for the organization rather than against it.

To motivate workers to the greatest extent possible, to encourage legendary performance, the leader measures workers' performance so that they can see whether they are achieving the desired results. Managers who do not do this run the risk of making the job description nothing more than a laundry list of isolated activities and negate the point of defining results in the first place. Having no means of telling whether they are succeeding, people in traditional environments lose interest in their jobs.

Weaknesses of Standard Performance Measures. Many managers who do measure performance tend to measure the wrong things; they keep track of hours worked or miles driven or client contacts made. These measures tend to lack meaning, however, because they do not really tell us whether the staff person or volunteer is accomplishing anything of value. They are not really measures of whether the result is being achieved. Standard performance reviews are both stressful and meaningless because they either measure personality traits (such as drive, tact, creativity) or whether a certain set of activities has been performed (such as numbers of reports completed on time). Measurement of personal qualities is always a subjective judgment that can be argued and that can form the basis of successful employee lawsuits. ("My boss didn't give me a raise because he said my judgment was poor, but he only said this because his judgment is poor, and he can't judge me accurately.") Measurement of whether activities are performed doesn't assess the quality of the performance.

A few years ago, I joined the board of directors of a nonprofit organization and was informed at the first board meeting I attended that the agency was experiencing a $30,000 budget shortfall. I asked whether the job of development officer, which appeared on the organization chart, was vacant. I was informed by the executive director that the position had been filled the previous January and that the person was doing a wonderful job. "Really," I said. "How much money has she raised?"

"What do you mean?" the executive director asked.

"You said she is doing a wonderful job. How much money have her efforts brought in?"

"Well," replied the director, "apart from our usual United Way allocation, she hasn't actually brought in any additional money as yet. But she really is an excellent employee. She works so hard. She writes the best proposals. She knows what the foundations are funding. She keeps up with what's happening. And she's very bright and pleasant. She's a great addition to the staff."

The difference in perspective here is an important one. The director was assessing this person's activities and personal qualities. Evaluating people's performance on these bases might reveal that they are very creative and inventive in the methods they employ, that they show drive and perseverance, that they get along well with others, dress appropriately, and put in more than the minimum number of hours. And, indeed, effective leaders might encourage their people along some of these same lines. However, such leaders would be concerned about these matters only because they may affect their people's ability to produce results. From this perspective, I had to conclude that the development officer was not performing her duties well at all and that the executive director should have talked to her about why her efforts were not bringing in any money. The director should have helped her decide to try something else. When people are immersed in activities, performance failures are often invisible and opportunities for growth are overlooked.

This may seem like a pretty tough approach, but the only reason leaders hire a person—unless they are running a charity program—is to get results. And measuring the worker's success in producing those results is the only meaningful way of assessing his or her performance. By creating results-based systems of measurement, leaders create a different relationship between the supervisor and the employees. In standard management, the pressure to perform comes from the supervisor. Because it comes from without, employees tend to resist such pressure. It helps them protect their sense of self-worth to resist it. When an employee finds that his performance is going to be measured in a meaningful, objective way, however, the pressure to perform comes from within. To protect his sense of self-worth under this type of system, he seeks to perform as well as possible, and when he isn't doing well, he naturally looks for help. The natural place to turn is to the supervisor.

Establishing Effective Performance Measures. To avoid the pitfalls of standard performance measures, leaders must know how to measure results and also how to set targets that prevent results from being interpreted as absolutes that are impossible to attain. To determine how to measure progress toward a given result, leaders involve the people who do the job. They ask them these two questions:

1. What information will tell us whether you are succeeding in achieving the result?
2. How can we collect the information?

This process may take an hour or two, but omitting it is to throw away a powerful management tool. When a worker knows the bases on which he will be judged, he will meet those criteria if he can control the actions that make that possible. If he is not doing well, he will naturally try harder to make sure he succeeds. Another way of stating this is that one gets what one measures. If one doesn't measure anything, one may not get anything.

At the same time, leaders must be careful about what criteria they set. One state government manager, for example, was told that he was not doing a good job because he gave too many outstanding performance awards. The concern of his supervisor was that he was cheapening the award and making it less meaningful. The manager was told that in the following year he was not to give more than 10 percent of his people awards for outstanding performance. This was a matter in which the criterion for his performance was clear and under his control. To get a good rating himself the next year, he didn't give any outstanding performance awards.

For some jobs the measure of performance is fairly obvious and easy to state. Imagine, for example, a crime prevention team in a police department that is striving for the result of keeping the neighborhood residents safe from burglaries. In this case, the number of burglaries in the team's area is a readily available statistical measure. By giving the team the challenge of reducing the number of burglaries, the leader gives team members a yardstick for assessing their performance. Every time a burglary occurs in their area, they will ask what they could have done to prevent it. This in turn will spur their creativity and encourage new and increasingly effective approaches. If the job is merely defined as engraving social security numbers on people's stereos and the team is given no feedback on how well it is doing, there is little likelihood that the team will come up with more effective approaches.

Sometimes the job may seem difficult to measure at first but turn out to be relatively easy. This was the case in the earlier example of the hospital food service workers who were responsible for seeing that patients found their meals appetizing. The information that would tell them that the result was being achieved was the opinion of the patients. Once that was determined, it became obvious that the way to gather the information was to ask the patients whether they found the food appetizing. Accordingly, a rating card was prepared on each patient's tray, and patients were asked to rate the tastiness of each meal on a scale of 1 to 7. Their answers were tabulated and each meal received a score.

The workers began to notice that some of the meals got high scores, while other meals did very badly. The workers then began to visit the patients to ask how the meals could be made more appetizing and received useful feedback. Some of the changes they made in response to these suggestions resulted in better scores, and a few actually made the scores worse. By retaining suggestions that worked and discarding those that didn't, the workers steadily made the meals more appetizing.

The measurement of other results requires more work. In the case of the Girl Scout leader whose result is to help her girls develop self-assurance, the leader needs to do some hard work to figure out how to measure progress toward this goal. She must ask questions such as "How will I know if girls gain self-assurance? What will I see if they are and are not self-assured? What questions can I ask them to determine their degree of self-confidence?"

Many leaders don't want to do this much work, so they take the easy course of holding their people accountable only for performing a set of activities (if they hold them accountable at all). By doing so, however, they deprive their paid staff and volunteers of the ability to tell how well they are doing. They also deprive them of a sense of accomplishment.

The second step in establishing effective measures of performance is setting high but reasonable targets. In this context a target is a goal of how many, how much, or what percentage the employee will try to attain during a given period. The target keeps the result from being interpreted as an absolute. For example, the result that some mental health counselors were trying to achieve was that their clients would return to independent living in the community. If we were to demand 100 percent, perfect achievement of this result, we would succeed only in frustrating the counselors. By setting a target of, say, getting one client back to independent living in the community each quarter, we do not negate the fact that our ultimate goal is to achieve this with all clients, but we hold the counselors accountable for a more realistic goal.

Targets need not be the same for all employees doing the same job. In the case of the counselors, for example, one may have several clients who have only mild difficulties, and for whom the goal of a return to independent living is relatively easy to achieve. That counselor should have a much higher target than one who has only very severe cases.

Targets should always be proposed by employees. If their supervisor believes that a particular target is unacceptably low (or unreasonably high), she or he can always disapprove it and ask for a more reasonable one. The reason that it is important for the employees to set the target is that they tend to resist or resent a target set for them by someone else.

To help employees feel free to set challenging targets, managers must make clear that failure to achieve one will not be cause for punishment. Rather, the manager's response to failure to reach a target should be the same as a golf coach's response to a player's failure to reach par. That is, the manager should go over the employee's work record with him, help him see why he did not reach the target, and help him learn from the experience so that he can do better in the future.

Setting targets too low, on the other hand, takes the challenge out of the job. To keep job interest high, leaders should encourage their people to set increasingly higher targets. This produces steady improvement in performance and, as the higher standards are achieved, enhances workers' self-esteem.

By establishing a system in which employees set challenging but achievable targets, leaders ensure that their employees will perform many of the tasks that traditional supervisors wind up doing, such as recognizing when things are not going well, determining what changes need to be made, and deciding how to make them. In this way, leaders help establish a climate that builds workers' self-confidence and self-esteem.

Measuring Legendary Performance. Measuring performance makes possible the setting of records. Records are tremendously motivating. People daily do ridiculous things to set records, such as walking backward for 1,500 miles. Why do people participate in such voluntary activities? For only one reason—to set a record. If people are willing to spend time and effort on useless achievements, think of the productive work they might do if there were records to set in their organizations. The impact of this can be seen in those few public and nonprofit organizations that have bothered to keep track of worker performance. Think back to the example of the state revenue department that greatly increased its collections simply by keeping score. In addition to motivating people to do a little better than they had before, the measurement of delinquent accounts also made it possible for the revenue officers to set records. At this writing, one revenue officer holds a record of 0.125 percent delinquent accounts. This is a record of which he is justly proud. It is the equivalent of Wilt Chamberlain's record for most points scored in a single basketball game.

Putting It All Together

In this chapter, we have examined three elements of exciting jobs—responsibility, authority, and accountability. If workers have jobs that embrace all three of these elements plus ownership (discussed in Chapter Five), they have a strong base from which to grow. Of course, finding interest in work is also an individual matter. Even if a job has all of these elements, some people will not enjoy doing it. Just as some people love bowling and others hate it, and still others are indifferent to it, so people will react to the same job in different ways. For this reason, managers must also be concerned with matching people to jobs that appeal to and motivate them. But first and foremost those jobs must include responsibility, authority, accountability, and ownership. If leaders omit any of these elements when designing jobs, the work structure will be unstable.

Chapter Seven

Developing
High-Performance
Organizations

For people to achieve legendary performance, they must be able to act quickly and effectively. When the organization's structure gets in the way of achieving the organization's purpose, people's commitment to that purpose wanes. In recent years, consultants, professors, and researchers in the field of management have urged a new management philosophy, one that is people oriented rather than procedure oriented, one that fosters a respect for the judgment and ability of the individual. However, many of the organizations that have tried to adopt this new philosophy have failed to make any corresponding change in their organizational structure. I am referring here to the kind of structure designed to operate according to an earlier philosophy, with an emphasis on single-skill jobs and strict management control, the kind of structure that promotes the commitment-destroying systems described in Chapter Five.

As we saw in Chapter Five, when responsibility is fragmented, everyone can point the finger of blame at someone else when things go wrong. No one seems to have the power to make things better. Leaders today inherit structures that have institution-

119

alized this fragmentation and make it impossible for people to be proud of their work. Many problems in large organizations turn out to be caused not by the people but by the way the hierarchy forces them to relate to each other. In fact, it is frequently true that the people somehow manage to make an ill-designed structure work better than it should.

Reducing Layers of Supervision

Too many layers of supervision lead to a lack of worker authority and responsibility. Government is particularly infamous for having more layers of management in one small agency than there are at General Motors. The purpose of so many layers is purportedly to ensure that no mistakes are made. To the worker, all these layers say, "We don't trust you to do a good job, so your work must be checked and rechecked."

Such systems of work organization also sap the commitment of managers and reduce productivity. One middle-level manager in a vocational rehabilitation agency once complained to me that his work load was killing him. We were in his office and he pointed to a huge stack of folders sitting on his desk. "Some days the pile gets bigger instead of smaller. I'd like to do something creative, but I'm too busy trying to reduce the size of this pile," he said.

"What do you do with the folders?" I asked.

"Well, those are case files. I have to review the dispositions that have been made and approve them," he replied.

Here was a case in which the bulk of a person's job was built around not trusting the person who made the original determination. In this case, it was also built around not trusting the worker's supervisor either, because each of the files had already been reviewed by the worker's direct supervisor. This system reduced worker and supervisor commitment, slowed service to the client, and wasted the talent of a highly intelligent manager.

Leaders free such people. They let them act. Effective leaders know that supervision is expensive and should be kept to a minimum. The point of supervision, in general, is to make sure other people do the work well. The more people there are doing the actual work rather than making sure other people are doing it, the more efficient the organization becomes. Each time a person checks up on someone she supervises, it takes time away from doing the work that the organization is there to do. In a lean organization, workers are empowered. The functions that managers fill their days with—the planning, deciding and evaluating—are done by the workers themselves.

Such an approach carries the risk that people will make mistakes. However, leaders are willing to take that risk, viewing mistakes as an opportunity for people to learn and grow stronger. Leaders, in fact, relish risk. They know that without it work becomes uninteresting and legendary performance is impossible. According to Andrew Grove, president of Intel Corporation, "Output will tend to be greater when everyone strives for a level of achievement beyond his immediate grasp, even though trying means failure half the time. Such goal-setting is extremely important if what you want is peak performance from yourself and your subordinates" (Grove, 1985, p. 165). Organizations that create layers of management to minimize risk doom themselves to mediocrity.

Traditional managers believe that managers should make all decisions. This philosophy denies the worker the authority to think and creates a need for more supervision. The number of people one manager can supervise depends on how much of the manager's time each individual takes. Grove (1985, p. 66) believes that on average an employee or equivalent takes about half a day a week of a manager's time. The amount of a manager's time any individual takes, however, varies inversely with the amount of authority to think that that person has. If the manager tries to direct the actions of the individual rather than allowing him to make his own decisions, the manager will have to spend more time in supervising those actions. If there are eight workers in an agency, one supervisor cannot effectively make all of their decisions for them. Traditional organizations therefore hire two supervisors. The work of these two in turn must be coordinated, so the traditional organization hires a manager to do this. Thus the multilayered structure grows.

Such organizations frustrate and isolate those in leadership positions. Every potentially decisive blow the leader strikes gets muffled and distorted by the thick layer of padding it must travel through to reach the people who do the work. Workers' ideas and concerns are beaten to death on their way through the jungle of approvals that separate them from the leader. When action is stalled in layers of approval, the purpose of the organization is frustrated. Leaders know that commitment stems from a sense of contributing significantly to a worthwhile purpose. Layers are therefore the enemy of commitment, an enemy against which leaders must take action.

Leaders lay the foundation stones of a streamlined structure by designing jobs that provide employees responsibility, authority, accountability, and a sense of ownership. This in turn results in fewer layers of supervision. Where jobs are designed in the traditional manner, streamlining will fail.

A city parks department had a maintenance division that employed fifteen full-time people—a director, a secretary, two foremen, an inspector, and ten maintenance workers. In the summer, when park use was at its peak, the department hired twenty additional workers, mostly high school students, to help maintain the thirty parks.

Each day, the inspector visited several parks and made a detailed analysis of the maintenance needs of each. The level of detail is indicated by the workers' nickname for him: "the little Nazi." Near the end of the day, the inspector returned to the office and reported to the director. Together, they set priorities and decided which workers would do what tasks the next day. Dividing the workers into crews was complicated by the seniority system. The most senior worker always got the most desirable job, and the least senior person was always assigned the least desirable job (such as rest room maintenance). This meant that the inspector and his boss often worked late to figure all this out.

When the workers reported to work the next day, they were told what they were to do that day, who would be supervising them, and in what park or parks they would be working. Ordinarily, each foreman supervised more than one crew. They would each get one crew started on a task and then go to a different park to get another crew started. In the summer, a foreman might have as many as six crews to supervise.

The foremen's major complaint was that when they returned to a work site they often found the crew sitting in the truck drinking coffee. When they asked why they weren't working, the workers' answer was that they weren't sure how the foreman wanted them to go about a task, or that they weren't sure whether he wanted something else done, or that they were done with the first task and were waiting to be told what to do next. "Oh, you're back," a worker might say. "It's about time you got here. We were waiting for a decision from you. We had a little disagreement about whether you'd want us to install this new bench parallel to the sidewalk."

Citizens sometimes complained about seeing workers goofing off in this manner, and some employees were found drinking beer instead of coffee and were suspended. The foremen urged their boss, the director, to get a budget increase to hire at least one more foreman so they wouldn't be "stretched so thin." Each complained constantly that "these idiots are driving me crazy." Both had ulcers.

Other problems included absenteeism and constant grievances filed by the workers. Absenteeism caused delays most mornings because the director had to readjust the composition of the crews to accommodate unexpected absences. A crisis occurred when the division's budget was cut by $50,000. Some of this could be saved by putting off purchases of new equipment, but the director was faced with the difficult prospect of cutting the two maintenance workers with the least seniority. He saw all sorts of morale problems resulting from this because those who were retained would have to do the less desirable jobs they had escaped years before.

In many such cases in government, managers are tempted to punish the public for not providing enough funds. Another park official, for example, responded to a similar situation by deciding that because of the budget cuts, rest rooms would be cleaned only once every two weeks and trash would be collected less frequently. Such a solution, while not desirable, not only solves the budget problem but sometimes puts so much pressure on the city council that the funds are restored.

This director, however, was dedicated to providing necessary services to the public, and he approached the problem from this point of view. This director was a leader, not a bureaucrat, so he first divided the workers into two-person teams and let all ten full-time workers divide the parks into five groups that required approximately the same amount of maintenance work. The teams bid on the "packages" of parks according to seniority. The director then gave the teams a clear definition of what constituted a well-maintained park and the authority to decide what to do each day in "their" parks. He also gave the entire group of ten workers responsibility for the complicated task of scheduling the use of scarce equipment so that each team could accomplish the desired results. This gave them the responsibility for three typical thinking tasks that are the exclusive preserve of managers in traditional settings: planning, organizing, and evaluating. Each month the teams met to review any scheduling problems that had occurred in the previous month (evaluating) and to develop a schedule for the coming month (planning). Further, in the summer, each team had the responsibility of supervising two high school students, which meant deciding how to deploy their work force (organizing).

Once this streamlined system was in place, it became apparent that, far from needing additional foremen, none were needed. In fact, there was also no need for the inspector, whose previous duties were deciding what needed doing and scheduling the work. When the workers themselves were given these responsibilities, the division suddenly had a manpower surplus on its hands.

At the outset, the director was concerned that those who had worked up to the more desirable jobs would resist having to do the less desirable ones. When he voiced his concern, however, the second most senior worker spoke up. His voice quaking with emotion, he said, "I will support whatever you decide, but in my job, most days I tighten bolts on the playground equipment. I have counted, and there are 2,014 bolts I have to tighten. I'd love to clean a rest room now and then."

The foremen and the inspector were initially skeptical about whether the streamlining would work. Even the director had been known on occasion to refer to some of the workers as "dumb as a stump." His skepticism in this case was overridden by a passion to continue to provide good service to the public and his willingness to take a risk, hallmarks of a leader.

Each worker began to take more pride in his work. Absenteeism dropped almost to zero. The appearance of the parks improved. Grievances against management disappeared, and a new sense of team spirit prevailed. One worker even brought his edger from home (the department didn't own one) to cut the grass back from the sidewalks in "his" park. This new attitude came as a welcome surprise to upper-level managers in the department, many of whom had referred to the workers as "the losers." However, the problem was not that the workers were losers but that they formerly had nothing to win in their jobs with the exception of the daily, ulcer-producing game they played with their foremen. Streamlining the organizational structure not only led to less need for management effort but to opportunities for workers to experience the pride of achieving something. By redefining the job and letting the workers decide how to distribute the work, the director was able to ensure better results with less cost and less management effort.

Such a system is not the norm, however, and even when it works, people used to the old ways of doing things are not comfortable. In this case, the maintenance director eventually retired. His replacement, a self-described manager of the old school, was "appalled at the lack of management control" being exercised in the system he inherited. "The next thing you know, they'll be having the city attorney type his own documents and the secretary trying the cases," he exclaimed. As times were better and there was more money to spend, he reinstituted the foreman system and then became exasperated at the deterioration of the quality of the work.

Separating doing from thinking is a subtle form of fragmentation of responsibility. Rejoining the two is not always easy. One city transit system, for example, had a set schedule for maintenance. When a bus had been driven a certain number of miles, the maintenance foreman tagged it for whatever services it needed. Workers were told what to do to what bus. None of the foremen could think of a better way to do this, although they acknowledged that the workers did not have the authority to decide what to do. After hearing the story about the park maintenance unit, one foreman suggested that the workers be assigned a group of buses that they would be responsible for maintaining. This did not seem practical, however, because the maintenance needs of one group of buses might occasionally be far greater than those of another. A lead worker came up with the idea of giving the individual maintenance workers groups of buses to track, with the goal of increasing the number of miles between emergency repairs. This did not mean that

Figure 7.1. An Overmanaged Organization.

only that mechanic worked on his or her buses—the schedule was too complex for that. However, mechanics could call up the maintenance records of their buses on a computer screen and also ask the drivers how the buses were doing. They could note recurring problems and warn a fellow worker of impending problems with one of his or her buses that they had serviced. And they could pull a bus out of service to work on it as they saw the need.

Increasing the Span of Control

When workers' jobs are designed according to the principles discussed in Chapters Five and Six, managers are able to supervise more people. A rule of thumb in streamlining an organization is that one person can oversee between eight and ten employees or do the equivalent. By doing the equivalent, I mean participating in task forces, dealing with external entities such as legislative bodies, and so on. A person who supervises five employees, for example, might also staff a citizen's advisory committee, have responsibility for communicating regularly with the news media, serve on an ad hoc task force, and have ongoing responsibility in drafting legislation in concert with a legislative committee. These other responsi-

Figure 7.2. Technical Supervisors of Technical Specialists.

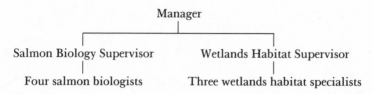

bilities would add the equivalent of four people to the person's supervisory work load.

Because of such external responsibilities, people at the top of organizations may supervise only one or two other people. When a middle-level manager supervises only one or two other people, however, alarm bells should ring.

Figure 7.1 shows part of the organization chart of a county public works organization. The fact that the lead workers in the maintenance division (who supervised the twenty-seven-person work force) were separated by two layers of management from the director of their division produced communication problems and delays. The deputy division manager and operations manager represented unnecessary layers as they had few "employee equivalents" to supervise. To streamline the organization, a leader would reallocate these positions to nonsupervisory work.

One exception to the one-to-eight or one-to-ten rule occurs when the work of a small group of technical specialists must be supervised by someone with a knowledge of their technical specialty. Figure 7.2 shows a portion of the structure of an environmental organization that illustrates this exception. Although the manager might be able to supervise all seven technical workers in terms of management control, it is unlikely that she would have the required expertise in both technical areas (salmon biology and wetlands habitat) that need to be supervised. Suppose that the manager is a technical expert in wetlands habitat only. In this case, the structure could be alternately streamlined as shown in Figure 7.3. Here the manager would also be a technical supervisor of the three wetlands habitat specialists and a middle manager of the four salmon biologists of the organization.

Such exceptions to the one-to-eight rule should be more com-

Figure 7.3. Streamlined Portion of the Organizational Structure.

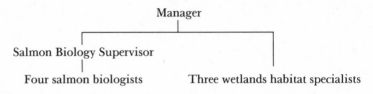

mon for first-line supervisors than for middle managers, however. The middle manager's role should not be one of providing technical expertise to workers. That is a supervisory role, and middle managers should give their people full authority to manage themselves.

The number of people who report to one manager can be increased dramatically in cases where work teams are established. One manager can supervise eight work teams almost as easily as eight individuals. In the parks maintenance case reported earlier, five two-person teams of workers reported to the director of maintenance. This was not the equivalent of ten people reporting to the director. He reviewed progress or received suggestions from a team just as he would from an individual worker.

On the other hand, managers generally expend more effort in managing a team than in managing an individual. They may, for example, have to mediate in conflict resolution, make sure that team members continue to act as a team, and so on. However, they will still spend less time doing these things than they would in managing each worker separately.

Keeping Staff Positions to a Minimum

One symptom of an ineffective structure is a high ratio of staff to line workers, those who do the mission-related work of the organization and the people who are in the chain of command above them. Those in staff positions include administrative assistants, members of planning departments, and others who provide support services.

Staff positions tend to be occupied by people who make high salaries. Much of the work they do is necessary only because the organizational structure is inefficient. One state agency, for example, found a project mired in the cumbersome communication and turf battles of the functional departments that had to work together on it. The agency hired a project coordinator to facilitate communication and provide direction. She did her work well, and it produced a better product more quickly. If the organization had not separated the people into different units to begin with, however, the coordinator's work would not have been necessary.

Leaders take a hard look at every staff position in their organization. For each, they ask whether the staff work could be performed by the line workers instead. Leaders also look for situations where staff people's actions frustrate the people on the line. Do line workers greet the annual plan with complaints, for example? If so, leaders ask whether the planning assistant or planning department is really necessary. Could the line workers and managers do the planning? If so, would their work be more whole and more satisfying? If the answer to these questions is yes, leaders free the line from the shackles of the staff directives, and put the people employed in some staff positions to work in more productive capacities.

For example, one-third of the employees of a government agency in an eastern state worked in a bureau of planning. Each year these employees worked long hours to produce an annual plan that the people in the bureau of operations were to follow. The planners did not consult the operations people when creating the plan. This immediately caused the operations people to view the plan with suspicion. Moreover, because the people in planning were unaware of the day-to-day realities confronted by the people in operations, the plan usually sounded good but was marginally relevant to the work to be done. As a consequence, the people in operations tended to ignore the plan. It would have been much more efficient to move some people from the bureau of planning to the bureau of operations, thereby expanding the services the organization could render and allowing people in operations to spend part of their time creating a plan that would be relevant and that they would follow enthusiastically.

Reorganizing a Matrix Structure

In a matrix organizational structure, people in staff positions have the equivalent of line authority over workers, thereby producing a

situation in which workers have more than one boss. This is particularly prevalent in government agencies where local, regional,
and headquarters structures exist. It is often the result of separating
the responsibility for planning and policy-making from the responsibility of doing the actual work of the organization. For example,
a state's department of employment services had twenty-seven local
field offices, most of them organized at the top, as shown in Figure
7.4. (Employment services helped people find work, unemployment
insurance provided federal and state compensation to workers who
had been laid off, and special programs dealt with job training for
the chronically unemployed.)

The twenty-seven local employment service offices reported
to headquarters through three regional offices, which were organized as shown in Figure 7.5. The three regional office managers in
turn reported to the agency's associate director for field operations,
a person who was supported by a staff of seven.

We can already see the typical and unnecessary propensity of
government organizations to create deputy positions at all levels. Although this is a structural weakness that cries.out for correction, the
real nightmare begins with the headquarters structure, shown in Figure 7.6. The associate directors for unemployment insurance, employment service, and special programs made policy in these areas, policy
that was supposed to be implemented by the local office managers.
These three associate directors also received and controlled the federal
funds the agency used to support these programs.

In such a structure, the people who implement the policy
have no voice in making the policy. As a consequence, policy often
fails to reflect the situation in the field. Field people in this particular organization would complain to their regional managers, who

Figure 7.4. Local Management of a Department of Employment Services.

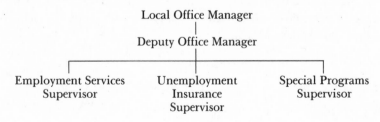

Local Office Manager
|
Deputy Office Manager

| Employment Services Supervisor | Unemployment Insurance Supervisor | Special Programs Supervisor |

**Figure 7.5. Regional Management Structure
of a Department of Employment Services.**

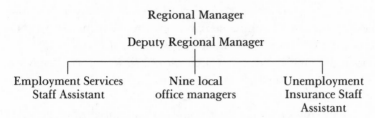

Regional Manager
|
Deputy Regional Manager

| Employment Services Staff Assistant | Nine local office managers | Unemployment Insurance Staff Assistant |

**Figure 7.6. Top Management Structure of a
Department of Employment Services.**

Agency Director
|
Deputy Director

| Associate Director for Field Operations | Associate Director for Unemploment Insurance | Associate Director for Employment Services | Associate Director for Special Programs |

would complain to their boss (the associate director for field operations). But although their boss had line authority over the people who carried out the program, he had no authority over those who made the policy. Political battles thus raged among the associate directors, who all were trying to get the agency director or deputy director to take their side. In such conflicts, there are winners and losers. Losers tend to lust for revenge. As a result, the purpose of the organization gets lost in vengeful politics and commitment is destroyed.

A leader who wanted to free the local office people to do their work could have reorganized the agency by vesting all funding and policy-making power in the line. The staff people would then have no direct policy-making power but rather would be consultants and assistants in the making of policy in their special areas. One way to do this would be to give the field operations associate director some staff to assist him with policy development. Another would be to give the deputy director of the agency the responsibility for field operations and have the three regions report directly to her.

The three remaining associate directors in that case would head small staffs to assist the deputy in providing direction through the regions to the local offices. However, the associate directors would have no authority to make demands on the local managers. The effect of either solution would be to invest the line people with the authority to make the policy that would govern their behavior. They would thus be freed to concentrate on giving the best possible service to citizens.

Sometimes matrix organizations are produced when generalists do the work and there is a desire to back them up with technical resource people. These resource people often have the authority to make policy. In a natural resources agency in a western state, for example, workers in the field had a strong sense of ownership and their morale was relatively high. Each one was responsible for one geographic area of the state. Within that area, a worker's activities included leasing state lands for mineral extraction and for agricultural purposes and overseeing the planting, maintenance, and harvesting of timber.

In the headquarters of this agency, there was a separate division for each of these activities, one for mineral leases, one for agricultural leases, one for timber, and so on. Each unit played a management role with respect to the field personnel, setting goals and standards and monitoring progress toward fulfilling them. Each made its set of demands in isolation, not knowing what the other units were requiring of the workers. To return to the letter mailing analogy in Chapter Five, it was as though a worker would not only fold, lick, and stamp while being supervised by the person in charge of a zip code area, but also would receive directives from divisions that specialized in folding techniques, licking techniques, and stamp placement. As a consequence, the workers felt as though they had several bosses. This caused confusion, and the line supervisors were forced to devote a great deal of effort to sorting out conflicting priorities.

One of the reasons that matrix structures create problems is that the people in the functionally based divisions of the organization have no direct connection with its product. To gain influence over the end product and acquire a feeling of efficacy, managers and staff of these divisions tend to vie with those of other units, sometimes in vicious political battles in an attempt to enlarge their territories at the expense of the other units. To go home at the end of the day feeling that they have made a contribution to the organization's product or purpose, they create rules that the people who actually do the work must follow.

Such organizations get bogged down in endless meetings to coordinate, to harmonize, and to solve problems of communication that the structure creates. Task forces are formed, staff members are hired to expedite matters, and new layers of management are added in an attempt to coordinate and expedite. People in these jobs work long, draining hours, often with the help of large staffs. They do perform a very important function, to be sure, but it is a function made necessary by the inefficiency of the organizational structure. It is a function that is totally unnecessary in a product-centered or results-based organization.

Streamlining in a Large Organization

Large organizations are, in theory, more efficient than small ones. In practice, however, they are often unwieldy, slow, and rife with "useful" but unimportant activities. Imagine, for example that you are the owner of a business that supplies office equipment to a government agency. When a new opportunity arises or a better way of doing things occurs to you, you can move instantly to seize the opportunity or to improve your effectiveness. Now imagine that you are an agency purchasing manager with those same responsibilities. Before taking action, you must wait for approval and perhaps become involved in political infighting with other managers.

Leaders who want fast action must therefore treat the large organization as a loose collection of small shops, each of which is led by an "owner" who is authorized to act, guided by the values of the organization and by a clear set of objective performance standards. Good leaders free their people from bureaucratic restraints.

Add up the number of people who actually do the work in most agencies (those who actually repair the roads, counsel the clients, and so on) and then add up the number of people in management, staff, and support positions. The ratio in large organizations is typically weighted heavily in favor of the "nonproducing" and, incidentally, highest-paid employees. What additional price is added to the service because of the business trips, meetings, and unnecessary approvals of these highly paid but not directly productive people? How many clients are not served because the organization's resources are spent adding such commitment-destroying positions instead of hiring people to provide more service? How many nonprofit organizations, such as a museum in my hometown, go deeply into debt, putting their services at risk, during the same year that they add a layer of supervision?

The inefficiency of large superstructures counteracts and sometimes outweighs the efficiencies of the large organization's economies of scale. For example, one large agency decided to give managers authority to buy anything that cost less than $50 directly from a retailer because the overhead of the purchasing department placed a $50 extra charge on anything they bought. The large, results-centered organization has both the competitive advantage of a lean superstructure and the competitive advantage of economies of scale common to all large organizations.

Product Responsibility

A large organization that operates on effective principles blends the advantages of bigness with the creative, motivational, and other advantages of small shops. One of the ways it does this is by creating a structure that is based on product managers and in which individual workers are totally responsible for the quality and quantity of production.

The first step in streamlining, then, is to identify the product of the organization. It is often eye-opening to make a chart that tracks the work flow and all the actors necessary to produce the product. The chart shown in Figure 7.7 tracks all the handoffs necessary to produce a timber sale by the natural resources department discussed earlier. Each number on the chart corresponds to a step in the timber sale process, from collecting forest inventory data to administering the timber sale contract. Eight organizational entities are involved in the twenty-three steps of this process. The process leaves one unit and goes to another seventeen times. To

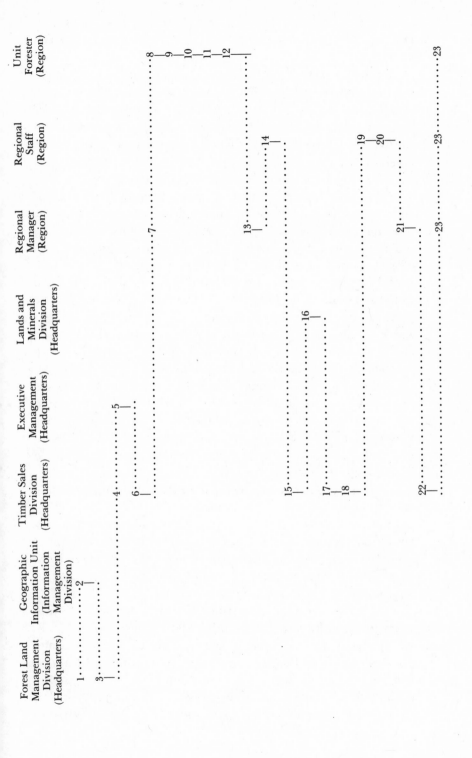

streamline this process, a leader would consolidate as many of the steps into one unit as possible so that responsibility for the final product (the sale of timber) would be housed in one unit. The leader would also direct the middle manager in charge of the process to consolidate responsibility for the various steps in as few hands as possible.

Organizing around a product is very different from the standard approach. Imagine a small tutoring agency that has a director and one worker. The worker recruits students and volunteer tutors, arranges for facilities, sets up a schedule, trains tutors, and provides recognition to volunteers. Imagine further that its program is a rousing success. The firm hires another person. At this point, a fateful decision must be made: what will be the job duties of the two workers? The traditional answer would be to have one person do the volunteer-related activities, while the other recruits students, sets schedules, and arranges for facilities. The product-oriented answer would be to have each staff person do all the activities for two separate groups of students and volunteers.

Imagine that the tutoring agency took the traditional approach. As its program continued to expand, the number of activities staff members performed continued to shrink, until finally one person did all the volunteer recruiting, another did all the scheduling, and so forth. Eventually, the seven staff divisions shown in Figure 7.8 were created.

The volunteer coordinator did all the recruiting, screening, and matching of tutors and clients. The marketing division recruited students. The materials section reviewed high-interest, low-level reading materials for use in tutoring. The tutor trainers trained the volunteers. The administration division enrolled clients, leased space, and so on, and the operations manager scheduled tutors and clients at the firm's various centers.

This standard functional approach to organizing work produces fragmentation of responsibility and all the attendant problems we have been examining. In our example, the structure creates possibilities for conflict between materials selection and training and between marketing and administration. It requires endless coordination and communication. No staff person has full satisfaction of seeing people learn. The structure also creates confusion in

Figure 7.8. Upper Management of a Large Tutoring Agency.

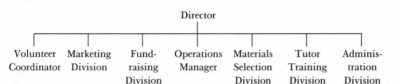

the volunteer tutors, who do all the work of the organization. One person recruits volunteer A, another trains volunteer A, and a third assigns volunteer A to a client. If volunteer A has a problem, to whom does he talk? Who gives him ongoing management support?

In streamlining this organization, the leader should try to get as close as possible to the purely product-oriented approach by heading each tutoring center with a staff person who performs all the program functions. This would create a confederation of small programs, each of which would have the freedom to experiment, to try new approaches. "But that would mean a lack of uniformity!" cry traditional managers. Exactly. Rarely is excellence a product of an emphasis on uniformity. We can only learn from people who do things differently than we do, so leaders should encourage people to explore new approaches and share what they learn with the others. Excellence is an ongoing process of experiment and growth. As the several tutoring centers share the successes and failures of their various attempts, each will adopt the best ideas of the other. Each center will be made stronger by the diversity of experiences of the others. As long as the client is well served, the leader should not be concerned that people are achieving this result in different ways.

Another objection to the product-oriented way of organizing is that it is inefficient to have, for example, seven different recruitment or marketing efforts. The resources of one center might not be sufficient to advertise the program effectively to potential clients and volunteers. While this may be true, rather than hiring an additional person to act as a recruiter, the leader can bring all the center directors together and have them plan a recruitment drive, pooling their talents and resources. In other words, the staff functions can be performed by the line people themselves. This saves the cost of hiring an additional person and gives the line people more ownership of the process.

In this case, there may be some activities that are clearly inefficiently provided by a large number of centers. Having so many centers would perhaps lead to variable efforts and inefficient use of personnel. Large, traditionally structured organizations often "solve" this problem by having a person run a program but be responsible to a program (or center) manager of operations and also to the divisions of training, recruiting, and so forth. Instead of creating line authority for such positions, however, it is better to have such divisions serve in a consulting capacity. This enables the content experts to spend their resources wisely and allows the center manager to make individual variations in the center's program. The authority is all in the line.

With some highly technical functions, on the other hand, organizations are better off with an internal source of expertise. Leaders in large organizations must wrestle with the best means of providing that internal service.

Internal Customer Service

Often we think of customer service as being something that we do for people outside the agency. In large organizations, however, many units have customers who are internal, who are other employees of the organization. It is here that customer service is often the worst. Recently, I did a study of the effectiveness of a large state agency. One of the questions I asked was, "Are there organizational improvements you would suggest?" I expected answers that highlighted inefficiencies in the system. Many answers expressed extreme frustration with the internal service groups, such as purchasing, media production, and equipment replacement—for example, "Drop a bomb in media production."

Internal service units generally have a monopoly on the business of their customers. As Albrecht (1990) points out, however, such units can generate "invisible competition" in the form of their frustrated customers trying to avoid using the service. Such attempts tend to create turf battles that waste the time of the organization and divert people's attention from the purpose of the group. In short, they destroy commitment.

People in such units usually don't want to provide poor service. But with only a fragment of responsibility and little or no authority to make decisions that serve customers, they can do little to control the quality of the service they provide. As Schlesinger and Heskett (1991, p. 73) note, management may blame the workers for doing a poor job, but "what is astonishing is that these service failures . . . have been designed into the system by the choices senior management has made."

Options for Internal Service Delivery

Internal services can be delivered to employees in any of five ways. The most obvious is one in which a separate unit of the agency provides the service—a typing pool, a contracts office, a purchasing department, a library, a computer systems division, or an engineering unit. There are inherent weaknesses in such units, all of which pertain to the loss of ownership on the part of the people who work in them.

Such units often produce slow and inadequate service. As David Osborne (1990, p. 22) suggests, "If policy makers can 'buy' services only from their own bureaucracy, they become captives of sole-source, monopoly suppliers. . . . We all know that monopolies protect inefficiency and resist change. And yet, to this day we deride competition within government as 'waste and duplication.' . . . It is one of the enduring paradoxes of American politics that we attack monopoly so fervently when it appears in the private sector but embrace it so warmly in government."

Other units of an organization frequently spend much time trying to evade the requirements of central units. This wastes energy and eliminates commitment. In one state agency, for example, people develop the reputation of being good managers if they can figure out a way to get around the constraining rules of the civil service system so that they can hire competent people. Others are congratulated for figuring out how to provide training without going through the central training unit. Such efforts arise because the employees of centralized units are often rewarded for activities other than serving the customer. A purchasing department employee, for example, might be rewarded for getting the best price, not for purchasing a quality product that pleases the customer. Another problem is that the employees of the central unit have no sense of ownership and responsibility for results. We will return to this problem later in the chapter. Right now, let's examine the four alternatives to this centralized approach.

The second way to organize internal service delivery is to have the customers provide the service themselves. This is the best way to deliver service when the skill required is not too technical and when giving the employees that responsibility creates more ownership and more pride. It also frequently increases efficiency. In the state department of natural resources discussed earlier, for example, foresters filled out a form to request new batteries for their flashlights. A study showed that it cost the department $50 in staff time for every purchasing request the purchasing unit processed. Obviously, this drove the cost of a flashlight battery to an astronomical level. The foresters were therefore given the authority to buy batteries at a local store. By avoiding the purchasing unit in this case, the employees got supplies faster and the department saved money. The department also found that the employees were more satisfied with the quality of the batteries they purchased themselves.

Automation provides many possibilities for providing a service for oneself. A bridge designer in a highway department, for example, can use computer-aided design software to produce drawings rather than sending her notes to a drafting unit. An appraiser can enter his figures directly into the computer as quickly as he can write them down on a form for someone else to key in later. An executive can type her own correspondence on her computer rather than writing it out in longhand and giving it to a secretary to type. What's more, the executive can then immediately make revisions on her own screen instead of waiting to get the document back from the secretary. Leaders might therefore empower people to perform the service themselves rather than set up a centralized unit.

The third way to provide internal service is to have it done by specialists in the organization's divisions. An organization with five divisions, for example, might have a purchasing specialist in each division. This is still a monopoly, but the specialist is more likely to be responsive to internal customers because he is supervised by the same person who supervises those customers. Poor service will then have direct consequences in terms of performance review, advancement, and other rewards. For example, if a computer system does not do what the employees need it to do, they will complain to their bosses, who will have the direct authority to order a revision of the system. In a central programming unit, on the other hand, political battles might well ensue, battles in which the director of computer services defends the programming ability of his people against unreasonable complaints from his peers. This third method is best used when the service is needed frequently by the division and the skill level necessary to providing it is high.

The fourth way to provide internal service is to have it done by a central unit but to designate which people within that unit will be responsible for serving which particular division of the organization. In this case, the specialist is supervised by the director of the service unit but is responsible for dealing with one particular customer. This method has an advantage over the third method when standardization of service is necessary.

The fifth method is to contract for the service. This method is becoming increasingly popular and may be the wave of the future. In this case, rather than having a central payroll unit, for example, you contract with a payroll company. The advantage is that you can take your business to a different company if you fail to get good service. This is often cheaper because the contractor may offer economies of scale unavailable to your organization.

One interesting variation on this fifth method is to allow your own central unit to compete with private providers. In Phoenix, for example, the public works department bids on the garbage collection contract against private haulers. It doesn't always win. In pursuing this variation, however, you need to make sure that all parties play by the same rules. In Oregon, when the state's industrial insurance department was allowed to compete with private insurers, the private insurers offered lower rates to the lowest-risk customers, thus saddling the state with the higher-risk customers.

To avoid this, the law could have required any private insurer to offer the same rate to all customers.

All these alternatives notwithstanding, leaders can make central units effective through the application of good job design principles. Where there are a number of specialized tasks to be done and where the volume of work from the internal customers is variable, leaders may opt for this approach. By offering people who work in such units a well-designed job, leaders can ensure that such units are much more effective than is normally the case.

Shortening the Chain of Command

In shortening the chain of command and simultaneously placing decision-making responsibility at or closer to the level at which the organization's work is done, leaders not only reduce overhead but create opportunities for more worker motivation and greater organizational effectiveness. This doesn't necessarily mean laying people off, however. The changes described in this chapter can be incorporated gradually, relying on retirements to eliminate positions without eliminating people. Those in management and staff positions can also be assigned to more productive work. In the park maintenance illustration given earlier, the director was able to transfer the younger foreman to a supervisory position in a different part of the department. The other foreman was given the option of early retirement.

Sometimes employees have the feeling of being frustrated by a long chain of command when in fact few layers of supervision exist. This happens when their work products must be approved by other employees who are not in the line of supervisory authority. Employees are kept waiting while their products languish in a technical department or on an individual's desk. Here the frustration stems from chains of approval rather than chains of command.

The message of this chapter is that effective leaders free people from wasting their energy in bureaucratic procedures. Many of these procedures are a direct consequence of the way the organization is structured. People waste their efforts in extra steps caused by layers of managers who must approve actions and by fragmented units whose efforts must be coordinated. The ultimate in streamlining the system is tearing down the entire hierarchy.

Ken Soldt, a senior manager at the Washington State Department of Natural Resources, believes that people of goodwill can make any organizational structure work. The implication is that people can and often do circumvent the established communication channels and structure to get the work done. Good leaders are on the lookout for this, not to quell it but to take advantage of it. They use the informal system as a road map for reorganizing things.

For example, imagine a unit of state government that produces maps of the state. Some of these are topographic maps; others are specialized geographic maps showing mineral deposits, income distribution, or annual rainfall. Some of the maps are drawn by hand. Increasingly, the maps are produced with the assistance of computer technology. The unit is supervised by a cartographer with no computer background. Computer expertise in the organization resides in the information management division.

In traditional organizations, the supervisor is regarded as the source of technical expertise. In this case, however, the technical expertise the workers need is in another unit, which has no cartographic knowledge. Traditionalists might move the cartographic unit into the information management division to try to supply the expertise. Or the workers in the cartographic unit could become "customers" of the information management division, waiting for service along with other customers. Leaders who want to get things done would tear down the functional hierarchies.

Effective leaders look at the skills that are necessary to producing a product or service and create a team with all the relevant expertise. Such teams may be temporary, disbanding once the need for the product or service is satisfied. However, the team members are not then reassigned to a functional unit. They become members of a new team. Rigid hierarchies must give way to teams of people from various disciplines working toward common purposes. These teams must be given full responsibility and authority and held accountable by regular progress reports.

In streamlining an organization's structure, however, leaders must be wary of allowing the effort to become an end in itself. As consultant John Carver (1990, p. 62) says, "Streamlined efficient structure is to be admired and much sought. But an organization neither deserves points for it nor loses points for lack of it. Whether an organization is good or bad is revealed in the results."

PART THREE

BRING OUT THE BEST
IN YOUR PEOPLE

Chapter Eight

Creating and Instilling Meaningful Values

Underlying the purpose of the successful organization is a set of values, a set of beliefs that drive the action of its people. These values contribute to the level of success the group enjoys. Without mutually agreed upon values, disagreements surface among workers, and people wind up working reluctantly on things that do not match their own sense of what is right and proper. The right values, internalized by each group member, lead to right actions on the part of the organization. Creating, articulating, and promoting these values is the responsibility of the leader.

I define values in this context as a sense of what is right and what is wrong. Examples of organizational values include providing good service to the client, taking initiative, accepting responsibility, doing only your best, and being committed to growth, win-win thinking, or innovation. Peter Senge calls values, mission, and vision the three "governing ideas" of an organization. According to Senge (1990, p. 224), "Core values answer the question 'How do we want to act, consistent with our mission, along the path toward achieving our vision?'"

The difference between values and slogans is that values guide the action of each group member. Unlike slogans, values are internalized. At a department store with a reputation for customer service, for example, I recently observed a man return a pair of shoes that the store had never carried. Even though he had not purchased them at this store, the clerk cheerfully gave the man a refund. The clerk did so because according to the values of the store, it was the right thing to do. Customers are to be served when they want to be served (which is why this store has more salespeople than other stores of a similar size) in the way they want to be served. For the clerk to have said, "I am sorry; we don't carry that brand" would have been wrong in this organization.

The clerk also made the decision to give the customer a refund without getting approval from higher authority. Internalized values enable the employee to make decisions. When managers are confident that their people know what is right, they can trust them to make decisions. Most organizations do not have clear values of this sort. In other stores, for example, the clerk might have been confused about what to do about the customer's request to return the shoes. He might have gone to his supervisor, who might also have been confused. The right and wrong things to do would not have been obvious.

A couple of years ago, a man wearing a gun came to the reception counter at a state personnel office. He asked to see the director of the department of personnel. The clerk told him he was at the wrong building and give him directions to get to the right office. He thanked her and left. After he was gone, she began to worry about the fact that the man had a gun and wondered if he was perhaps a mentally unstable, disgruntled job seeker. She wasn't sure what to do, however, and went to talk to her supervisor. He wasn't sure what to do either. Should they call the director's office and warn him? Should they call the police? Eventually, they went to the supervisor's boss. After some discussion, she decided to call the police. The police found the man sitting in the chair of the fortunately absent director, gun drawn, waiting for the director to return.

As illustrated in this example, when employees don't know what to do, they tend to ask their supervisor. This involves the supervisor in the details of an employee's job, diverting the supervisor's attention from her or his own work. It is difficult to lead when your attention is immersed in the work of those you are leading. It also takes more effort to manage when you are embroiled in making case-by-case decisions. If the decision from one case is inconsistent with a decision in another case, the values are further blurred. When the line between what is right and what is wrong is hazy, it is hard for group members to know when they are stepping over the line. It is also harder to bring someone who is behaving inappropriately back to the right side of the line when the line itself is unclear.

Organizations that have no clear set of values tend to rely on standard operating procedures and policies to make sure people do the right thing. Where there are no guiding values, procedure manuals are very thick. Whenever someone does something stupid or a crisis arises, managers in such organizations write a new procedure to prevent its recurrence. Because no procedure ever covers all eventualities, the procedures themselves can lead to irrational actions.

In 1990, a blizzard of unusual severity struck my hometown of Seattle during rush hour. Gridlock ruled the streets. With visibility close to zero, cars inched timidly along the steep hills. It took many people over an hour to travel a single block. On the bridge connecting the city to Mercer Island, a bus full of commuters came to a standstill. As the storm abated, the passengers noticed that people had abandoned their cars and were walking past the bus. The passengers asked to be let out to walk across the bridge to their homes. The bus driver refused to do so, because they were not at a bus stop and the procedure manual clearly stated that he was to let people out only at official stops. He held the increasingly irritated passengers hostage for hours, finally delivering them to their stops after the traffic got moving again.

In most cases, stopping only at bus stops is a good rule. If every passenger could get off the bus wherever he wanted, service would be slow. Moreover, a passenger successfully sued the transit company ten years ago when a driver granted her request to be let off between stops and then she slipped and fell. Nevertheless, such slavish devotion to "the book" is the deadly enemy of a leader of a service organization. The procedure manual replaces the employee's own best judgment. It creates poor service and low morale. It tells employees, "We don't think you are capable of making an intelligent decision." It robs them of the authority to think, increasing stress, resentment, and apathy. Employees will be more capable of outstanding work if they are allowed to make their own judgments within the framework of clear organizational values.

When we speak of values, we are talking about the culture of an organization. Traditional managers regard such matters as values as too ethereal. "We're hard-nosed here," the president of a small company once told me. "I expect my workers to do what they're told, when they're told to do it, in the way they're told to do it. If they don't like it, they can go down the road." This person then went on to lament the poor quality of work he got from his employees. Effective leaders realize that culture is extremely important. By putting an emphasis on creating a culture that carries with it positive beliefs about the capabilities and qualities of each member of the organization, effective leaders help each person come to believe that she or he possesses those capabilities. If a worker believes that the other workers in his agency do superior work, he will be more likely to believe that as one of the workers, he should produce superior work, and this belief will drive him to strive to do so.

Today many organizations are wisely trying to create a sensitivity to cultural diversity. There is much to be gained in terms of mutual understanding from such attempts. Good organizations, however, cannot afford to have competing sets of values where work ethics and client service are concerned. In an increasingly pluralistic society, leaders will take charge of individuals from different cultural backgrounds. Sensitivity to those backgrounds is important in understanding who those people are. The organization's culture, however, must guide the work life of its people, all of whom must be committed to one set of work values.

Deciding What We Stand For

All this means that the manager who wants to build a truly outstanding organization needs to go beyond the important questions of "What are we trying to achieve?" and "How will we achieve it?"

to the questions of "Who are we? What do we stand for? What do we believe in? What are the characteristics of our organization? What does it mean to be one of us? What kind of person is lucky enough to work here?" These questions ought to be considered frequently by every leader, and the positive answers to them should be broadcast frequently to the employees to help create a strong sense of the group's standards and traits.

Although the primary responsibility for establishing shared values is that of the leader, it is best to involve the followers in delineating what these values are. Using questions such as those just posed, the leader needs to lead the group in a discussion of what principles the group believes should guide its actions. To do this means looking at the organization's mission and vision and its relationship to its clients. This also involves looking at the strategic plan and asking what principles of behavior would most effectively guide the organization in the pursuit of those goals.

One way to help a group identify positive values is to ask, "How would you evaluate an organization with a similar mission to ours? What criteria would you use? What kinds of characteristics would the employees have? What would constitute an excellent organization?" These questions will elicit many overlapping characteristics. Leaders often group similar characteristics into broader categories. For example, if the group comes up with characteristics such as caring, concerned, and dedicated to clients, a leader might group them into the larger category of being service oriented.

Once these broader values have been developed, leaders ask the group to make a commitment to them as guiding principles. Leaders ask whether group members are willing to help build an organization that operates according to these values. Although it is unlikely that anyone would say no to such a question, some people might suggest barriers that could make it difficult to live up to the values. For example, if the group decides that it is important to project a positive, caring attitude toward clients, someone might point out that the burdensome, bureaucratic procedures of the organization make service slow and inconvenient for clients. They might say something like, "It is difficult to project a caring attitude when people are frustrated by filling in the same information on twelve different forms in four different locations." Leaders welcome such suggestions because they point out areas in which the system can be improved. Once people see that positive changes are being made to help make the values a reality, their enthusiasm will increase. People get excited about being part of an excellent organization.

The values should support what the organization is trying to accomplish. In nonprofit organizations and government, that frequently means providing some sort of assistance to a client or citizen. One powerful way of looking at that assistance is to see it as a promise from the agency to the client. The leader might therefore stimulate a discussion of values by asking what it is the organization promises to the people it serves.

This kind of discussion has the advantage of connecting the values of the organization to the mission. If the mission is to ensure a safe and stable home for every child in the community, for example, the promises of the organization might include, among other things, the following:

> We promise children of the community a home life that is free from physical and emotional harm.
> We promise to provide knowledge of the child development process to parents in the community.
> We promise to help parents in the community develop skills in dealing with their anger and to understand the consequences of their behavior.

These promises should then guide the behavior of the employees and managers of the agency, and daily decisions should be shaped by the promises. In such circumstances, people go to work to keep a promise rather than to reduce the paper in their in-baskets.

Acting on Our Principles

More important than deciding on a group of abstract values or principles, however, is helping people achieve a clear vision of how they can translate those values into actions. Too often, top management develops value statements, announces them, and assumes that members of the organization will automatically act on them. Because there is often a lack of communication between top management and those doing the work of the organization, these assumptions tend to go unchecked. As a consequence, there can be a great difference between what management assumes is happening and what is really happening.

Leaders must make clear what the values mean in practice and empower people to behave in accordance with them. As Larry Combs, a vice president of marketing for Parker-Hannifin, once told me, "Telling people we expect them to make a contribution to finding better ways of doing things does no good unless we also show them how to find such ways and how to communicate their ideas."

One of the best organizations I have ever been involved with as a consultant is the fire department in Kent, Washington. It has always been a successful department with high morale, but in the last few years it has become one of the best fire departments in North America. One of the reasons for this relates to an event that happened in 1988. With the help of a consultant, the top management of the city developed a statement of values for the city. This statement was entitled "Kent Cares," and it contains five basic values— community service, commitment to results, valuing people, team actions, and innovation. Each value is followed by a statement of core beliefs, such as "We take risks and make changes to improve service" and "We pride ourselves on high production and quality results balanced with a concern for people and process." The statement is intended to guide city employees in their dealings with the public, and the fire chief, Norm Angelo, puts a lot of stock in "Kent Cares."

At a planning retreat in 1988, I asked the fire department participants to introduce themselves and to explain what "Kent Cares" meant to them. As we went around the table, the top brass of the department had glowing things to say about what the statement meant to them. Then we got to John Willits, the union president. He said, "To me, the 'Kent Cares' philosophy is just a piece of paper. It's a joke. It doesn't mean anything."

I had to admire Willits for his courage in making this statement in a room full of gold badges. I also had to admire the leadership for the way they responded to his statement. Lesser people would have reacted defensively, accusing the union president of trying to make trouble. At Kent, the leaders reacted by saying, "We have a problem. If the people who deliver the service aren't living these principles, then we ought to do something."

Chief Angelo did something that very few other fire chiefs would do. He held a one-day retreat for the twenty-seven lieutenants of the Kent Fire Department to discuss the values of the organization and what they meant in practice. This was an expensive thing to do, with two-thirds of the group getting paid overtime for their attendance and nine fire fighters being paid extra to serve as acting lieutenants for the day. Most fire chiefs wouldn't dream of spending all that money on something so airy as a discussion of values. The consequences of that meeting, however, made it one of the best expenditures the department ever made.

At the retreat, we reviewed the values and then spent the bulk of the day examining the question "If we believe in this value, what does that mean we do?" The lieutenants were asked, for example, what it meant to give the best service in the event of a fire. The first answer was to get there fast, put the fire out effectively, and get back in service quickly. We then looked at the "Kent Cares" philosophy statement that said, "We project a positive, caring attitude." How did that fit in? As the lieutenants began to explore this, they considered what might upset the citizen even though they had done their work quickly and effectively. If the citizen was dismayed by damage to the property done by the fire department, for example, they would not have acted in accordance with the value. So they decided that if the fire department really wanted to demonstrate this value, they would take the citizen through the property and explain why they broke the window, kicked in the door, or cut a hole in the wall and how those actions limited fire damage.

All day long, we talked about ways the department would act in terms of the "Kent Cares" philosophy. Ideas ranged from small suggestions, such as asking people standing at the counter if they have been helped, to larger suggestions such as calling heart attack victims after they returned from the hospital to see how they were doing, and explaining fire inspections as a free service to help business owners rather than a law enforcement operation. Other ideas included getting a radio station to donate small teddy bears that the department could give to children whose houses had been damaged by fire. The lieutenants then went back and talked to their companies about the ideas that came from the day's meeting. The next year, at the planning retreat with the same cast of characters, the union president gave his evaluation of what had transpired that year. He said, "We are living the 'Kent Cares' philosophy, and we know why."

Today the Kent Fire Department functions as a model organization. Never have I encountered an organization of any kind with higher morale, more pride, or a greater sense of commitment. It is a testament to the leadership exercised not only by the chief but throughout the entire department.

Training in Values

When most people think about training their volunteers and staff, they think only about the skills required by the job. Those who are more aware also provide training in self-esteem and personal development, knowing that the more confident their people are, the better their organization will do. Very few organizations, however, provide training in the area of values. Such training should describe the organization's values and suggest how those values can be exemplified in daily behavior. It should clearly give people an understanding of the principles of "right" behavior. To be effective, however, the training should deal with common situations in which members of the organization may have to make value-based decisions.

For example, as the trainer for the fire department described above, you might suggest the following situation: "You and your four-person engine company arrive at the scene of a heart attack. The victim is a sixty-year-old man who is unconscious. His wife is nearly hysterical with fear. Describe exactly what you would do." The discussion would of course include the emergency medical procedures the company would undertake, but the values-related discussion would revolve around what the engine company would do for the wife.

It is important to stress that such training does not seek to inculcate a standard procedure. The point of the above scenario is not to get people to conclude, "We always leave someone behind to comfort family members." Rather, a range of responses can be considered "right" behavior, as long as they demonstrate an appreciation of the value "We care about the well-being of the citizens of this city." A value-driven organization expects its people to make judgments about the best thing to do in a given situation on the basis of principles, not rigid procedures.

Reinforcing Values

Once the values are known and people have a clear sense of how to act on them, the leader's job is to reinforce the values, to keep them alive as a driving force in the group's behavior. Leaders do this in several ways, the first of which is by paying close attention to behavior that is in accordance with the desired values.

Paying Attention to the Right Things

Whenever leaders observe "right" behavior, they should acknowledge it. This acknowledgement can take the form of a smile, a nod, or some other gesture. In some circumstances, it might consist of oral, written, or symbolic praise as described previously. For example, at a job training center, a supervisor who placed a high value on taking initiative wrote a letter of commendation to a volunteer who had written and posted a sign that made it easier for applicants to figure out the process of registering for training.

Leaders make sure they know all the facts inherent in the situation so that their praise is meaningful, however. One county commissioner, unfortunately, did not. He learned that members of the county road crew did not feel appreciated. Knowing that they were building a new road, he went to the job site with a box of doughnuts and a large thermos of coffee. The crew appreciated the coffee and doughnuts, and everything was going well until the commissioner, who knew little about road building, told them that he appreciated the excellent job they were doing on the road. "Good job?" one of the men shouted. "This isn't a good job. This is a terrible job. We just graded this road last month. It ought to lie here for a year as a gravel road before it gets paved. This is all going to break up before the winter is over. We figure we're only doing this for political reasons. Was it you who decided we should pave this thing? Do you have a relative that lives on this road?''

When looking for behavior to praise, leaders must avoid undercutting the chain of command. When they see evidence of wrong behavior in someone they do not directly supervise, they should not comment on it directly. Corrective action is a management task, not a leadership task, and the matter should be taken up with and left to the worker's supervisor. This maintains the supervisor's responsibility for managing his or her group, and it helps save leaders from the embarrassment of jumping to the wrong conclusion.

On the other hand, if there are no intervening levels of management, leaders should quickly show their disapproval of wrong behavior. A mental health center director once hired a fiscal officer who had no mental health background. His office was near the client waiting room. On one occasion, he expelled clients from the waiting room because they were making too much noise, making them wait outside for their appointments. When a therapist informed the director of this, he commiserated with the therapist about the fiscal officer's inappropriate behavior was but took no corrective action. The director thus failed to enforce a widely shared value of putting the needs of the client above all other concerns. This weakened the director's influence over the staff.

Spreading the Word

In addition to paying attention to the right things, leaders reinforce values by spreading the word when the right thing is done. The leadership of the Kent Fire Department, for example, gets calls from citizens who are impressed by the service they have received from the fire fighters. For example, the chief might get a call from a citizen who expresses his appreciation for the fact that the emergency medical technicians saved his father's life. The citizen might also thank the department for leaving someone behind to calm and reassure his mother and for calling back later to see how the couple were doing and to wish them well. Chief Angelo spreads such stories at every opportunity. He lets people know what their fellow employees did, stressing that this is the kind of thing that makes the Kent Fire Department a very special organization.

Similarly, Laura Lee Geraghty, director of the Minnesota Office of Volunteer Services, keeps a "warm fuzzy file" of kudos received for the work of her staff and volunteers. When she receives a complimentary letter about one of her people, she routes it to all staff and volunteers working on the same project and includes it in her quarterly report to her boss and the advisory board.

Spreading myths can also be effective. Just as Knute Rockne rallied Notre Dame by creating a myth about "the Gipper," so too can effective managers help their people feel pride in and dedication to the values of the organization by relating stories that may only be loosely based on fact or even only on the spirit of the people involved. As a young executive once said to me of such myths in his organization, "If they aren't true, they ought to be."

In most organizations, stories are told, but they are often negative stories. In my consulting work, I hear such stories all the time. People talk about the time when someone successfully defied management's authority or about how demoralized everyone felt when executives got bonuses even though the company had suffered record losses. They talk about a time when someone was unjustly accused or about disastrous decisions or about the leader who continually and arbitrarily changed policy or about the time when someone went beyond the standard procedure to help a client and was reprimanded. Such stories poison the climate of an organization and make commitment impossible. Conversely, spreading positive stories produces a positive climate.

Measuring Performance

A third way of reinforcing values is by holding people accountable for accomplishing results related to the purpose of the organization and in accordance with the values of the organization. In other words, people's performance in exemplifying the values will be measured.

When leaders meet with their people to determine the means of measuring performance, they must keep the values of their organization clearly in mind. Criteria for measurement should lead to behavior that is in accord with those values. For example, a volunteer fire chief, whose department placed a high value on fast responses to emergencies, timed the responses and gave regular feedback on this to his several volunteer captains.

Similarly, one of the values espoused in an adult literacy program was that all personnel be sensitive to the potential embarrassment of adults in admitting that they cannot read. The director regularly solicited the opinions of the adult students on how comfortable they felt attending the program and kept track of the number of people who enrolled but did not show up for tutoring. Volunteer tutors were given access to this information so that they could tell how they were doing. As a consequence, they went out of their way to make sure that their clients did feel comfortable.

As emphasized in Chapter Six, leaders must take care in deciding what information to use to measure people's performance. People try to achieve the things that are measured. A bus driver, for example once called in on his radio to say that his bus had become stuck in the snow. Hours went by. When the stranded passengers asked him to call again, he said he couldn't do so because it was against the standard procedure to call more than once. To call a second time would be noted as a demerit on his driving record. After several hours, the passengers forced him to call a second time. When he did so he said, "I hope you realize I may never be driver of the year because of you people." Make sure that what you measure will result in performance that is consistent with the values of your organization.

Setting an Example

A fourth way in which leaders reinforce values is by acting in accordance with those values themselves. By setting an example of the kinds of behavior they expect from others, leaders provide a role model for others to follow. For example, a recreation leader whose organization put a high value on win-win thinking refused to accept a majority decision because part of the group did not support it. She instructed the group members to keep communicating until they had a decision they all felt good about.

On the other hand, leaders sometimes fail to live up to their own standards, to "walk their own talk." If a leader stresses punctuality in conversations but always starts meetings late, she is not

acting in accordance with her announced value. If a leader emphasizes the importance of the individual but never takes action on an
individual's recommendations and never gives individuals the authority to put their own ideas into practice, this puts the lie to his
espoused value. If the leader talks of the importance of taking initiative but then keeps a tight grip on things, telling people what to
do, she is not acting congruently. When followers see the leader
betray the organization's values in these ways, they will be unlikely
to take the values seriously.

The leader of one public health organization, for example,
talked a lot about the necessity of protecting the environment from
inadequate septic tanks. One of the complaints of the field staff was
that when they sought to enforce the department's regulations on
septic system design, often a citizen would complain to the leader
and have the regulation altered or waived. This incongruence between the leader's pronouncements and his actions created confusion among the staff about what was the right thing to do. In such
cases, morale suffers and the efforts put forth by the work force are
reduced.

One of the most important areas in which a leader sets an
example is that of work habits. If an organization is to prosper, its
members must focus their energies on the things that make a difference. If the leader is continually responding to crises, setting
priorities based on whatever is demanded from outside the group,
this behavior will encourage similar behavior in the followers. The
actions which make the vision a reality, the actions that require
proactive effort, will never be taken. Similarly, if the leader quits
when she senses difficulty, spends the first hour of the day social-
izing or reading the paper, hops from one project to another, puts
things off until the last moment, or regards the job as a backlog of
tasks to get through, she will fail to inspire her people to work at
full potential regardless of her rhetoric.

Good work habits that leaders should exemplify in their behavior include the following:

> Giving first priority to what will make the most difference
> Working diligently, with concentrated attention

Getting tasks done early; arriving early for meetings, appointments, and work

Having a well-organized way of dealing with paper

Having clear goals for the work day

Saying no to low-impact tasks

Common values can be further communicated through management's internal memos, daily announcements, and recognition of individual and group achievements. Leaders make sure that these routine means of organizational communication reflect rather than contradict the principles of the organization. If the value is innovation, and an innovative employee is passed over for promotion or not given recognition for his achievements, leaders put the lie to their statements.

Serving the Community

Yet another way that leaders reinforce values is by seeing that their organization takes congruent action in the community. A hospital that values the health of people in the community it serves might, for example, sponsor a drive to collect groceries for a local food bank. A community action agency might take part in a peace march. A utility company's environmental affairs division might participate in cleaning up a local hiking trail. Such actions are not directly related to the mission of the organization, but they say something about the values that the organization espouses. When those actions are congruent with the organization's values, they reinforce the sense of "who we are" and "what we stand for."

Directors of volunteers and development officers in nonprofit organizations can offer corporations opportunities to take similar actions. For example, corporations can be encouraged to allow their employees to volunteer in an agency or to donate money to it. The leader of an agency working on senior transportation, for example, might approach a local automotive business for volunteer help and support. By contributing to that cause, the business would be telling its own employees what it stands for and what is congruent with its mission. The Pillsbury Company targets its giving to groups that address the problems of hunger and homelessness because it is in the food business and to youth because the company employs many young people in its fast-food outlets.

Using Slogans

As noted earlier, values are very different from slogans. Nevertheless, slogans can be used effectively to reinforce values. At the Kent Fire Department, personnel wear buttons that say, "Committed to Service." IBM, in the early days of its success, was sometimes ridiculed by outsiders for the slogans that were plastered on its walls, but these slogans enunciated the beliefs that were adopted by the workers and helped make the company the formidable competitor it is today.

In service organizations, good slogans often involve a promise to the customer or client. The Federal Express slogan "Absolutely Positively Overnight" speaks volumes about what is the right thing for employees to do. If the hour is late and it is starting to snow and a Federal Express driver is wondering whether she should continue down a country road to make her delivery, that slogan, which embodies the company's promise to its customers, tells her that to turn back would be wrong. Similarly, a program working to reduce child abuse has a slogan "A safe and stable home for every child." As with employees of Federal Express, volunteers and staff can use this promise as a principle to guide them in thousands of daily decisions.

Similarly, the internal affairs unit of a state police department was (as is frequently the case with such units) not very popular with the rest of the department. Other officers regarded the unit as a threat. By making the promise "We guarantee fair play" its slogan, the unit gave itself a new identity with the other officers.

And finally, the Minnesota Office of Volunteer Services' slogan is "On the cutting edge of volunteerism." The leader makes sure that the people in the agency know that this means they are to try things and take risks to push the state of the art of volunteerism farther. If you can enunciate such a promise, refer to it frequently. Refer to counterproductive behavior as breaking the promise. Congratulate people for keeping the promise. Doing so will keep people focused on the purpose of the organization and reinforce a sense of values that is consistent with that purpose.

To summarize, leaders help establish and reinforce values by keeping them in front of people at all times. They reward "right" behavior, spread the word of that behavior, measure performance so as to hold people accountable for value-driven behavior, and make sure that they and their organization act in accordance with the values they and their people seek to exemplify. In doing so, leaders build a system based on values rather than authority. People do things because they are right, not because they were told to do them. In the words of Tom Peters and Robert Waterman (1982, p. 291), "Clarifying the value system and breathing life into it are the greatest contributions a leader can make."

Chapter Nine

Helping People
Grow

People work at their best when they are optimistic, when they are hopeful and feel good about themselves. Leaders who encourage legendary performance help their followers to be optimistic and to grow.

Dealing with Setbacks

One of the most important tasks in ensuring that people are optimistic is helping them cope with the inevitable setbacks the organization will encounter. As discussed earlier, people's ability to remain hopeful in the face of adversity is a product of how they explain the adversity. Seligman's research (1991) shows that two main variables determine whether people respond with hope or with despair to a setback. These variables are the degree to which people explain the setback as permanent or temporary and the degree to which they regard the setback as general or specific.

Suppose that a person in a nonprofit agency writes a grant proposal to fund important activities and the proposal is rejected.

If this person believes that the proposal was rejected because he is "not very good at writing proposals," he is likely to feel depressed and discouraged by the event. The next time he has to write a proposal, he will probably not be able to give it his best effort. The explanation is that he has a deficiency; it is a permanent condition. If, on the other hand, he explains the rejection by saying that he was too busy with his other work to write a good proposal, he views the setback as temporary and believes that he can do a better job next time.

If the proposal writer believes that foundations never like the proposals he writes, he is attributing his failure to a general, pervasive cause. It is not just this one foundation but all foundations that fail to appreciate his work. With such a belief, he will have a hard time generating enough confidence to pursue the next proposal enthusiastically. On the other hand, if he explains the rejection by thinking that this particular foundation didn't appreciate his specific ideas in this proposal, he limits the setback to this one situation and will be able to approach the next assignment optimistically.

It is the responsibility of leaders to help their people find temporary and specific causes for setbacks. In the face of adversity, leaders try to keep their people upbeat and optimistic. They talk to their people about the circumstance of the setback in terms that limit the damage to the temporary and specific situation. Permanent and general explanations of negative events lead to feelings of helplessness, which in turn produce negativism and depression. In talking to their people about mistakes, leaders need to help them see that they are not powerless but can do something about the situation.

It is hard to work at peak performance when you are depressed. Seligman (1991) found that people who felt helpless were lethargic and didn't think very clearly. Depression is also contagious. It can become pervasive in the organizational climate and reduce everyone's potential. In such situations, a leader's questions are more important than declarative statements. The questions leaders ask should focus others on what they can control in the situation. For example, imagine the leader of a nonprofit organization talking to the proposal writer mentioned earlier. In this conversation, the leader is careful to divorce the person's sense of self-worth from the proposal.

"How did things go on the grant proposal?"

"I really screwed it up. It was a disaster," replies the proposal writer.

"I'm surprised to hear that, Jim. Why do you say it was a disaster?"

"They turned us down. Some days I don't think I'm cut out for this job."

"Why is that?" asks the leader.

"I'm just not good at writing."

"I think you're being a bit hard on yourself. You've written many good proposals."

"Well, foundations don't seem to think so."

"All foundations?"

"Well, this one, anyway," says Jim dejectedly.

"What you're saying is that this foundation turned down this proposal, is that right?"

"Yeah."

"Was there anything good about this experience?"

"What do you mean? No. It was awful."

"Is there anything you could learn from this?"

"Well. Maybe. I'm not sure."

"What can you learn from it?"

By turning the employee's attention away from the fact of the rejection (a past event that he cannot now control) and toward what he can learn from it, the leader gets him to concentrate on something that he can control. If he dwells on the past, he will focus on something he cannot change. This helplessness leads to feelings of depression, as we saw in Chapter Three. Instead, the leader has him focus on positive action, on learning something that will make him more capable in the future. In this way, leaders promote a climate of growth, where setbacks are seen as learning experiences that make people stronger rather than as disasters that get people down.

Fostering a Climate of Growth

Workers' dedication to improving their abilities is the most valuable asset an organization can have. It is a product of two factors.

The first is knowing the extent to which they are succeeding. This requires that workers know the results for which they are responsible and that they get feedback on their performance in achieving those results. The second factor is that the workers know that the leader will regard a setback not as a cause for punishment but as an opportunity to help them improve. The leader will help them discover why their performance was not up to par and help them plan how to do better next time. The leader helps others succeed rather than trying to goad or coerce them into better performance.

As noted several times earlier, managers who seek to design fail-safe systems drain the life out of an organization. If an organization is to grow and prosper, people need to try new things. Some of them are bound to fail. Leaders delegate the right to fail to everyone in the organization, with one proviso: people must be willing to learn from their mistakes so that they will be able to do better in the future. Just asking someone what he learned from a setback, however, may not be enough. The person may be too depressed or frustrated to view the situation objectively. In such situations, leaders can help their people by guiding them through the steps to follow in learning from their experiences.

We often hear it said that people learn from experience, but in fact, they do not always. Many keep making the same mistakes over and over again or fail to profit from their successes. Further, in traditional organizations, one employee will often make a mistake that was made earlier by another employee. Using standard management techniques, supervisors must take pains to ferret out the reasons for the mistakes (which employees often try to hide from supervisors) and then communicate them to the rest of the group. Unfortunately, this often takes the form of creating new regulations and standard procedures that constrain people's creativity and reduce their enthusiasm.

Learning from experience involves three steps. First, we "identify" the experience; we do not learn from an experience unless we can describe it to ourselves or to others. Second, we "analyze" the experience; we think about why the experience occurred and why it had the characteristics it did. And finally, we draw some generalizations that apply beyond the single experience.

To help someone grow in the job, the leader should keep

these three steps—identify, analyze, and generalize—in mind and, at regular intervals, review the employee's experiences according to this three-step format. Such a review should not be rigidly bound to the format; the order of the steps may vary. By keeping the format in mind, however, the leader can readily facilitate an employee's growth while simultaneously monitoring progress and helping the organization get better results.

For example, let's return to the case of Jim, the person who wrote the unsuccessful grant proposal. The first task (as far as his growth is concerned) is to identify his experience. The leader therefore asks him to describe in some detail what he did. Jim says that since the agency serves youth, he went to the foundation directory and compiled a list of foundations that fund youth programs. He then wrote a proposal to one of them describing the mission of the agency, how the program he was describing fit the mission, and how much it would cost. Unfortunately, the foundation decided not to fund it.

The leader then asks Jim why he thinks this happened (the analyzing step). He replies that he doesn't know and complains that he worked very hard on the proposal and thought that the foundation would surely fund it.

"Put yourself in their shoes," the leader says. "Can you think of any reason why they wouldn't fund it?"

"The only thing I can think of is that I didn't do a good enough job of stressing the importance of the project," Jim responds.

"You said you worked hard on it. Did it seem to you that you stressed the importance of the project?"

"I thought so. But I guess I didn't get my point across."

"I think you're being too hard on yourself. Why did you decide to apply to this particular foundation?"

"They had funded some similar projects in the past."

"Let's suppose they did indeed see the importance of the project. Is there any reason they might not have funded it anyway?"

"I don't know. They funded three others."

"Imagine you were an officer in that foundation," suggests the leader. "You already have three similar projects going. What might cause you to decide not to fund another?"

"Maybe the others weren't working too well."

"Maybe. Anything else?"

"Maybe they wanted to do something different."

"Those are two possibilities. Is there anything you can think of that you might have done to ascertain this before you sent them the proposal?" asks the leader.

"I guess I could have called and talked to them," acknowledges Jim.

The analysis phase is now complete. The leader next goes on to see whether there is a generalization that will focus Jim on positive action. The leader asks, "Did you consider sending the proposal to any other foundations?"

"Yes, but they haven't funded anything exactly like this."

"On the basis of your experience with the first foundation, what can you do to improve your chances to succeed with one of the others?"

"I guess I could call and talk to them first, see if they're interested in the idea."

To make sure Jim is focused on action, the leader asks, "When will you do that?"

"I guess I could do it this morning," he responds.

Jim is now thinking in terms of positive action that he can control. He has profited from his experience and has become more capable and optimistic.

During such conversations, leaders may leap to conclusions and have the urge to tell an employee what to do to improve his or her likelihood of success. This may impress the employee with a leader's knowledge, but it creates feelings of dependence on the part of the employee. To help others maintain a positive attitude, leaders need to discourage such dependence. They need to help others feel effective and discover a productive course of action themselves. As a result, others will feel even better about themselves and be capable of more enthusiastic action.

Concentrating on the growth of one's people not only helps keep them motivated, but it helps make one's own job less frustrating. If managers concentrate directly on the output of their people, if that is where the managers get their satisfaction, then they will be frustrated as managers whenever their people are less able to do the work than they are. Standard management practice is born of this frustration, because when managers see that employees are less able to achieve results than they are themselves, they tend to handle their frustration in one of two disastrous ways: they either try to do the important jobs themselves, which overloads them and discourages the workers, or they attempt to control their people's behavior, which leads to resentment and apathy.

Odd as it may sound, results-oriented leaders do not focus directly on the results their people achieve. They do not get their greatest job satisfaction from their people's achievements. Such satisfaction is for the workers to savor. Rather, leaders get their satisfaction and avoid frustration by concentrating on the growth of their people. When leaders concentrate on this instead of on absolute success or failure, they are less frustrated by imperfect performance because they can get satisfaction from their followers' improvement. Leaders also become more effective because if their people are growing, getting better and better, the results the leaders achieve through their people will continue to improve. Leaders' primary product, then, is the growth of their people.

This does not mean that leaders have low performance expectations. In fact, they usually communicate the expectation that their people will achieve a higher than average level of output. When people work in organizations with low performance expectations, their morale and productivity plummet. As Tom Peters (1988, p. B6) argues, "Because our expectations are low, we create and perpetuate a vicious circle: Low expectations lead to low demands, which in turn lead to workers' mental retirement on the job." Leaders who want legendary performance must demand it. When it is not achieved, they should demand constant improvement. This means constant learning. People should know that any failure to meet the high standard will be greeted with a demand to know what they have learned that will make them more successful in achieving the expected level of performance next time.

There is a direct correlation between an empowering system and a climate for growth. As Senge (1990, p. 287) states, "Helplessness, the belief that we cannot influence the circumstances under which we live, undermines the incentive to learn, as does the belief that someone somewhere else dictates our actions. Conversely, if we know our fate is in our hands, learning matters."

Providing Validations

When leaders affirm permanent and general causes of a person's good work, they create a validating climate. Validations affirm another person's positive qualities. As such, they differ from recognition, which focuses on the behavior of the person rather than on his or her personal characteristics.

In their simplest form, validations begin with expressions such as the following:

> You are
> You always
> You can
> You do

These are followed by a positive quality the person possesses. For example, when someone comes up with a bright idea, we might respond by saying, "You are really smart" or "You always come up with the best ideas." Such statements make people feel good and bolster their confidence and self-esteem.

In our society, many people are uncomfortable saying, "You are" and following it with a positive. Many, in fact, have been formally trained not to do so. You may be more comfortable with another form of validation, making a statement about yourself and your reaction to the person being validated. Such statements may begin as follows:

> I admire
> I like
> I respect
> I'm impressed by

For example, you might say, "I'm impressed by the professional way you handle our clients" or "I admire the patience you show in frustrating situations."

The most important rule concerning validations is that they be honest statements, reflecting a sincere belief. If we tell a person who is chronically late that we admire his punctuality in the hope that the validation will change his behavior, we embark on a self-defeating course. For one thing, the people we supervise will already have well-developed beliefs about who they are and will tend to resist statements about themselves that run counter to those beliefs. Further, they will quickly conclude that we are trying to manipulate them, and their trust in us will evaporate. Those in leadership positions must retain the trust of their people. If they cease to trust, they will cease to follow.

Validating people's good qualities is easy. The challenge is to find some positive quality that a problem performer possesses and to encourage it. By validating this person's positive traits, leaders create good feelings. The person will want these good feelings to continue and may start to improve in other areas. When this happens, other honest validations can be given, and these will produce more good feelings. By using validation in this way, a leader can help turn a person's work life around. Such people will realize that their increased self-esteem comes from their relationship with their leader, and they will be disposed to continue to be committed employees or volunteers.

Let's look at an example of how all this fits together. Suppose you have a receptionist who often irritates you by taking inaccurate messages. The tendency in such a circumstance is to make all your interactions with this person negative. If you didn't think through the consequences, you might say, in exasperation, "You don't pay enough attention to the numbers people give you!" This is a permanent and general explanation of the failure. Instead, after thinking carefully, you say, "You didn't get this number right. What will you do in the future to do the kind of job you are capable of doing?" This gets the receptionist to focus on a specific and temporary cause of the poor performance and gives him a sense that there is something he can do to improve.

Meanwhile, instead of concentrating on the receptionist's negative behavior, you ask yourself whether there is anything praiseworthy about him. Suppose that after some reflection, you realize that he is very personable when he answers the phone. That afternoon, you say to him, "I admire the pleasant way you answer the phone, even late in a frustrating day. You always give people a positive impression of our agency." The receptionist feels good because of your validation, and the next person who calls will likely get an unbelievably pleasant and positive reception. Having been praised for a positive quality and focused on what he can do better in other areas, he may start to put more effort into taking accurate messages. Eventually, you will be able to say in all honesty, "I like the care you take in making sure every message is accurate." This is a permanent and general explanation of a positive behavior. It promotes good feelings and a desire to do good things. It builds self-esteem.

It is interesting that in our society, we are naturally adept at saying negative things that influence another person's self-image, but we are not used to making positive statements relating to that self-image. Whenever someone does a good job, we tend to say something about her actions, not about her personal characteristics. "That was good work you did" or "You sure did a good job on this" are just two examples. On the other hand, when someone does something wrong, we tend to talk about her personal characteristics, not her behavior: "How can you be so stupid?" or "You are the most unreliable person I've ever met," for example. While the former are fine things to say, such statements do not reinforce a person's belief that she possesses a particular positive quality. The latter statements, however, directly affect the person's self-esteem. They tell her that something is fundamentally wrong with her character.

Effective leaders turn this societal tendency on its head. To get top performance from our people, we need to help them develop a sense of personal competence. We need to help them develop a self-image that drives them toward greater performance and helps them grow. We also need to deal with negative behavior as behavior only, not as reflections of true character.

Here are three positive, personal characteristics we might like to see in our employees: being a self-starter, being reliable, and being creative. Try writing four different validations for each characteristic before reading the following suggestions.

Possible validations for the first quality, being a self-starter, include the following:

I'm impressed by the way you take the initiative on
important projects.

What a go-getter!

With a self-starter like you on our team, no one can stop us.

You already have things done by the time I think of telling
you to do them.

All of these validations speak about the employee's personal quality, not his individual actions. The second suggestion, for example,
talks about the kind of person the employee is, not that he got the
ball rolling one time on one particular project. The employee is
being told not that he did one thing right—which he may or may
not think is a fluke—but that he is the kind of person who assumes
responsibility consistently. This will give him a good and positive
feeling about himself, and he will begin to look for opportunities
to live up to that validation. He will look for opportunities to keep
that good feeling alive by taking the initiative on all projects. If we
continue to validate this quality, his belief that he is a self-starter
will become stronger and stronger. This is one way, then, in which
we can help our employees begin to achieve their full potential by
helping them build strong self-beliefs.

Let's look at other examples. Here are some possible validations for the second quality, being reliable:

I can always count on you.

I always feel confident when you're on a project because you
are so reliable.

You're as reliable as Big Ben.

I'm proud to have a dependable person like you on my team.

These statements are a bit more dramatic than the previous ones.
If your personality is such that you feel comfortable making such
statements, you may find them very effective. Because these statements are more likely to have an emotional impact, they are more
likely to affect the subconscious mind.

Here are some statements that affirm the characteristic of
being creative:

You always come up with creative ideas.

Whenever there's a new solution to be found, you will find it.

We're lucky to have a creative person like you on our team.

I never cease to be amazed at how you can view situations in new ways.

Holding Growth Meetings

One way in which some leaders attempt to maximize growth is to chair periodic growth meetings with the people they supervise. The frequency of such staff meetings depends on many factors, such as how important it is for employees to work together and how comfortable the leader is with their performance.

Individuals come to these meetings prepared to talk about what they have attempted to accomplish since the last meeting. If their attempts are successful, they get recognition from their peers. If not, they get sympathy. However, the purpose of the meetings is neither recognition nor sympathy; the purpose is learning. Members of the group are expected to analyze their experiences—both successes and failures—and to state what they have learned from them. Others can ask questions and also suggest what can be learned from the experiences. In this way, the entire team profits from the learning of each member, and the entire team grows. This emphasis on mutual learning brings people together. It keeps them from making mistakes that a co-worker has already made. People also learn how other group members succeeded and become more capable of replicating that success themselves.

Focusing on the Controllable

Leaders can also foster growth by seeing that their people focus their attention on the aspects of a situation or project that they can control. Most commonly, people focus on the things that they cannot control, and this produces feelings of helplessness, which in turn produce depression. Leaders turn this focus around.

For example, a leader might be greeted by an employee who

is upset with another employee and so says, "She was supposed to be here to meet with Mr. Jones, but I can't find her anywhere. I've called everyone I can think of to find her, but she's not here." In this simple example, the employee has exhausted all the productive actions he can take to get his co-worker to the meeting. By continuing to focus on what he cannot control, he is wasting energy and making himself feel increasingly impotent. It is up to the leader to direct the employee's attention to a more productive course of action. She might do this by asking, for instance, "In the time you have left, is there anything you can do to salvage the meeting? Given that your co-worker is not here, what can you do to make the meeting with Mr. Jones a success?" Such questions guide the employee's attention to what he *can* do. It makes him feel more powerful, more in control. He may still be unhappy with his co-worker, but his energies are directed to productive action rather than wasted in helpless frustration.

Dealing with Successes

Leaders need to approach their people's successes in a very different way than they approach their people's setbacks. One of the findings of Seligman's research (1991) on optimism and depression is that opposite types of explanation are in order when people succeed. It is important to make the cause of successes permanent and pervasive, not temporary and specific.

Imagine, for example, that the grant proposal discussed earlier is accepted. If the writer explains this by saying, "I finally got lucky," he is explaining his success as temporary. If he says, "They liked this proposal better than my others," he is explaining the success as specific. He will feel more successful and positive, however, if he explains the acceptance as permanent ("I am a good proposal writer") and general ("People always understand the importance of what I say in my proposals"). Again, leaders can suggest such statements to their people, or they can use questions to help their people focus on their successes.

Earlier, we looked at how important it is for people to view setbacks as an opportunity to grow, to become stronger. People can also learn from their successes. Let's return again to the case of Jim, the grant proposal writer. Imagine now that the second foundation to which he applies agrees to fund the project. After he recounts his experiences, the leader asks (to encourage analysis), "Why do you think you were so successful this time?" He responds that he applied the rule of sounding out the foundation before he wrote the proposal and that the strategy seems to have worked.

"Is there anything else that you've done differently?" the leader asks, returning to the identifying step. She does this because she wants to make sure that they don't lose something valuable.

Jim thinks for a minute, then says, "Well, I included an executive summary of the main points of the proposal at the beginning."

"How would that have helped?" (Back to analyzing.)

"Well, even though I talked to the foundation about the project, it was a pretty long proposal. I put the summary in so that people would see the big picture before they started reading the details. I thought it might help them understand it better as they read along."

"How else might it have helped in the long proposal?"

"I don't know," Jim answers.

"If you were reading several proposals, which would be more appealing, one with a summary or one without?"

Jim thinks again. "I guess it might be fairly difficult to grasp some of the concepts. And awfully overwhelming to have to read several long proposals."

"So it took less effort to understand your proposal."

"Right."

Now, for the generalizing part, the leader asks, "Based on this, is there any rule you can think of that you should follow in the future?"

"Always add a summary?"

"Something broader than that. A general principle that this is just one example of."

Jim thinks. "Make it easy on the proposal reader?"

The leader has now succeeded in helping the proposal writer learn something broad and significant from his success. She has helped him identify parts of the experience that might have otherwise been lost and helped him draw a particular lesson from them that might not have been learned. To make sure that Jim applies the principle, the leader might close the meeting by saying, "That sounds good to me. Think about other ways you could do that and try them out before our next meeting."

Chapter Ten

Creating a Positive
Organizational
Climate

The organizational climate—how it feels to work in a place—is something that traditional managers spend little time worrying about. Leaders, on the other hand, realize that the climate affects everything that is done in an organization in a subtle but important way. Good leadership enhances followers' self-esteem. It helps them experience themselves as important, effective individuals. For many people, however, the work experience is often numbing; at worst, it can be destructive of the individual's sense of self-worth, and this in turn affects the performance of the organization. If people feel irritated, angry, diminished, or depressed at work, they are unlikely to engage in legendary performance. Leaders correct this situation in part by creating a climate that allows people to feel they are accomplishing something of value.

In striving to build a positive climate, leaders need to pay attention to the demotivating effects of little things. As quality crusader Philip Crosby (1984, p. 20) says, "The actions that . . . create a negative atmosphere are usually not big items." Many little annoyances diminish workers' feelings of control over their environment and their work. For example, when a large nonprofit organization moved to a new building in Washington, D.C., in 1991, employees were told that they were not allowed to move the furniture in their offices and that they could not bring in their own lamps unless they had a note from a doctor. Further, they were not to hang anything on the walls of their offices. Such petty regulations reduce the workers' sense of control and communicate a lack of trust in their judgment, hardly a boost to their self-esteem.

Conditions Conducive to Self-Esteem

Effective leaders recognize the importance of creating a positive climate that enhances people's self-esteem. Psychologists Harris Clemes and Reynold Bean (1981) identify four conditions that contribute to self-esteem: a sense of connectedness, a sense of uniqueness, a sense of power, and clear ideals or models. All of these conditions are enhanced by effective leadership. Let's examine each one in turn.

Connectedness

Leaders create a climate in which people feel connected. Their people feel a sense of belonging, of being part of the group. This need for belonging and acceptance is one of the most important motivational needs that people have. In our highly mobile society in which friends often live hundreds of miles away and the next-door neighbor is a stranger, this need is often unmet, leaving people with a sense of isolation, dissatisfaction, and loneliness. Psychologist William Glasser (1984, p. 9) points out that this need is often stronger even than the need to survive in that most people who try to commit suicide do so out of loneliness.

The sense of identification with a work group, whether it be paid or voluntary, can meet this need for connectedness, producing healthier, happier individuals. As Robert McDermott, CEO of the United States Automobile Association, puts it, "Perhaps the most important factor in esprit de corps is being needed by the other guys in your unit" (Teal, 1991, p. 123).

In my seminars over the past two years, I have surveyed more than fifteen hundred individuals who at one time in their lives felt a positive sense of connectedness. The following were most often mentioned as factors in producing a sense of connectedness:

1. A common goal
2. Common values
3. Mutual respect
4. Mutual trust (safety to be oneself)
5. A sense that one group member's weaknesses are made up for by another group member's strengths

As discussed in previous chapters, leaders act to promote positive feelings of connectedness in the following ways:

- Leaders establish a common propose or goal for the group. Nothing is as fundamental to a group's effectiveness as a common sense of what the members are trying to achieve together.
- Leaders establish a shared philosophy and common values that form the basis of each person's work behavior.
- Leaders establish high performance expectations and standards. If the expectations are easy to meet, people will not feel special about membership.
- Leaders make jobs whole. Fragmentation produces distrust, blaming, and criticism, which are the enemies of connectedness.
- Leaders celebrate the accomplishments of individuals in light of their contributions to the purpose of the whole group. They make sure the recognition is consistent so that people do not suspect favoritism. They celebrate group accomplishments, giving credit to all members.

The following paragraphs discuss additional things leaders can do.

People with a sense of connectedness have a sense of "we" as well as a sense of "I." The more special the "we" is, the more special the individual feels as part of the group. This is why it is important to have high standards for becoming a group member. "I don't want people thinking they are part of an average group," one highly effective city department director said to me. "I tell people when I offer them the job that if they want to be an average employee, putting in eight hours of work for a day's pay, this is not the place for them. But if they want to put out maximum effort to accomplish something special and important, then they can succeed here."

Leaders should be on the lookout for comments people make about the expectations they have of themselves and their co-workers. If people say, "close enough for government work" or "this place is a zoo," it should cause alarm bells to ring. People's self-esteem plummets when they regard themselves as part of a below-average group. This negative sense of connectedness leads to high turnover of staff and volunteers. When leaders hear such negative statements, they get their people to focus on the positive by asking, "What makes you say that? What can you do to improve this situation? In what kind of place do you want to work? What can you do to make this organization more like the kind of place you want it to be?" By asking these questions, leaders empower their people to make positive change.

One of the subtle reasons for the success of outstanding organizations is that they have a strong sense of what is "like them." Leaders should spread the word of positive accomplishments. They should talk about the values and standards of the organization and what it means to be part of the group. Regardless of the personal beliefs-about-self individuals bring to the job, they will develop the positive traits the group possesses if they identify strongly with the group.

In fostering a sense of connectedness, leaders also look for opportunities to promote interaction among group members. This is particularly important in situations where there are few "natural" opportunities for people to share their common experiences. Several nonprofit groups, such as Senior Companions and Court Appointed Special Advocates (CASA), assign volunteers to work with clients away from the office on their own schedule. Volunteers work with little daily supervision and rarely appear in the office. Effective directors of such programs, knowing that "it's lonely out there," take pains to bring their people together for training, pot lucks, and the sharing of "war stories." One CASA group accomplished this and strengthened board involvement by having each board member regularly host a social gathering for ten volunteers.

Probably the surest way to promote interaction is by involving people in the decision-making process. When each group member feels that she or he has a say in deciding the unit's strategy, that member's sense of connectedness is strengthened. In the midst of this process, it is important that leaders not let their own biases and positions be known in advance. Group members who know what the people in authority want will tend to support that position. This does not breed true connectedness.

Leaders also create connectedness by spreading word of what individual volunteers and staff members have accomplished. Anita McGinnes, who works for the CASA program in Houston, spotlights six volunteers in each issue of its newsletter. Each volunteer tells what makes her or him proud to be part of the program. The newsletter goes to all volunteers and several thousand other people in the Houston area. The "CASA Proud" column builds a sense of "who we are."

Finally, people's sense of connectedness is enhanced when they engage in new experiences together. By insisting passionately on constant improvement, leaders encourage people to try out new ways of doing things. If the entire group participates in this, the sense of connectedness grows.

The need for connectedness is so powerful for most people that the work environment will never seem fully satisfactory without it. Turnover and conflict may result. As volunteer management guru Steve McCurley says, "The absence of connectedness either leads to people joining a different team or creating a sub-team which may revolt against the main group."

Uniqueness

The second condition that contributes to self-esteem is a sense of uniqueness, a feeling that "no one else in the world is quite like me." People who believe they are unique feel that they are special in some way, that they each have a unique combination of talents and personal qualities. Leaders encourage this sense of uniqueness by recognizing the achievements of individual group members and by validating their individual qualities. Leaders encourage their followers to express themselves and, by giving them the authority to think, to explore alternative ways of achieving their results. Leaders also enhance their people's sense of uniqueness by giving them

challenging assignments that take advantage of each particular individual's strengths. "This is a difficult responsibility requiring
your special talents," a leader might say. Such a statement, of
course, should always reflect a sincere belief.

The need to feel unique is sometimes in conflict with a person's need to feel connected. We all tend to make compromises in
terms of our uniqueness in order to feel connected and sacrifice
some connectedness in order to feel unique. Imagine, for example,
a staff person named Julie. Part of her sense of uniqueness revolves
around her image of herself as a free spirit. This manifests itself in
a variety of ways, such as her wearing unusual clothing and jewelry.
Her organization's values, however, are quite traditional, and it is
an accepted group norm to dress conservatively. Julie is faced with
a choice between dressing conservatively to gain a sense of connectedness, thus sacrificing some of her uniqueness, and continuing
to dress in her unique style and being a bit of an oddity to the group.
Neither of these courses of action is fully satisfactory to her. In a
truly positive climate, people feel safe to be who they are. They can
behave in an individual manner, respecting each other for their
unique strengths and eccentricities, and yet support and be supported by the group.

Creating such a climate is often difficult. It cannot be done
without a great deal of interaction among group members, shared
values, and a common purpose. In some cases, it may require the
services of an expert facilitator to lead a retreat in which group
members explore their differences and similarities. However, the
sense of uniqueness is always enhanced when leaders talk up the
strengths of individual members and their contributions to the purpose of the group. It is maintained when leaders regard as "wrong"
behavior one person making fun of another or disparaging the other's accomplishments or desires.

This sense is also enhanced when leaders encourage the individual development of each person by providing maximum training. A common way of doing this is to send people to conferences
and workshops to keep them up-to-date with the latest developments in their fields. Conducting workshops specifically tailored to
the needs of the particular organization is especially beneficial. One
of the most powerful ways to provide such training is to have in-

dividual group members research a topic and present their findings to the rest of the group. This enhances the presenters' feelings of uniqueness—they have special knowledge they are imparting to others—while also creating connectedness.

Power

The third condition that leads to self-esteem is a sense of power, a feeling that one makes a difference, that one is effective in interacting with the world. It is this component that traditional work systems most often throttle. If people work in fragmented systems, unconnected to a final product, it is difficult for them to feel that they are making much of a difference. The self-esteem of such people is reduced, and they feel alienated from the organization.

Many organizations get caught up in their procedures and blunt any feeling of power and effectiveness. I recently talked to an employee of a federal agency who was spending his days reviewing one-hundred-page documents that had been submitted by federal grantees. Each of the hundreds of documents contained mind-numbing details concerning the degree to which facilities are accessible to the handicapped in the agencies in which the grantees placed volunteers. Each grantee had asked the agencies to fill out the forms, noting the slope of ramps, the width of rest room stalls, and so forth. I asked him what would happen if he found that an agency was not in compliance with the regulations. "Would you demand they stop placing volunteers in such an organization?" I asked. "No," he said, "we just gather the information and compile it."

It is difficult to feel like a powerful, effective human being when your days are consumed with activities of so little payoff. Jay Hall and Susan Donnell (1988, p. 545) call the management style that produces a sense of impotence "not bureaucratic but *bureaupathic*; and the risk in government is that bureaupathic managers put pressure on otherwise normal and healthy subordinates to behave in pathological ways. Preoccupation with minutiae, strict compliance with procedural guidelines, precedence as priority, and impersonality, even when pursued for the sake of 'professionalism' are essentially unhealthy managerial tactics."

Part of feeling powerful is having a sense of being in control of one's life. Managers often take this away from their people by trying to control their behavior. Rather than defining results and allowing people some say in figuring out how to achieve them, managers tell people exactly what to do. When one human being attempts to control the behavior of another, the result is rarely top performance. Instead, managers reap resistance and apathy. As explained in earlier chapters, leaders produce feelings of power by defining mission-based results. They put people in charge of something meaningful. They then allow those people to control their own behavior by giving them the authority to think.

Sometimes, however, empowered people wind up acting in ways that diminish others' sense of power. As Steve McCurley once told me, "In a large, bureaucratic organization, when you put people in charge of something, they tend to make rules and procedures that demotivate others and waste their own time." Put a person in charge of office decor, for example, and he might create a committee to review the appropriateness of the things people use to decorate their offices. Such a system not only diminishes other people, but it is a waste of the committee members' time. Leaders therefore need to monitor the systems being put in place by their empowered people to ensure that they are not creating wasteful procedures. When they are, the leaders should intervene. Members of the organization should clearly understand that wasteful effort robs the people they are trying to serve.

Like the need for uniqueness, the need for power is often in conflict with a person's need for connectedness. People in groups sometimes yearn for more freedom of action. Their desire to influence others sometimes alienates other group members. They usually wind up compromising their need for power in order to maintain their sense of connectedness or vice versa. As Glasser (1984) points out, almost everyone goes through life tying to balance these conflicting needs, making compromises that are never fully satisfactory. If a leader can create a situation in which conflicting motivational needs are met simultaneously, she or he will unleash a tremendous sense of well-being and enthusiasm for the job. More will be said about this shortly.

Ideals

Clemes and Bean (1981) call ideals, the fourth condition contribut-ing to self-esteem, models. By this they mean that to have high self-esteem people need principles, standards, goals, images, and role models to guide their behavior. Leadership actions that enhance this condition include the following:

1. Leaders make sure their people have a clear goal to pursue, know they are responsible for achieving the goal, and can clearly visualize achieving it.
2. Leaders make sure everyone understands and can articulate a vision of what the organization is becoming.
3. Leaders define and enforce clear organizational values to guide people in otherwise ambiguous situations.

One of the reasons that people follow leaders is that leaders have attributes that followers value and want. Leaders provide a role model for followers. When leaders behave in accordance with pos-itive principles, their people develop mental models of behavior that guide them to better performance. For example, when leaders encourage their followers to ask, "What could I do today that would make the most difference?" instead of "What is the most urgent thing to do today?" they help their followers create a proactive mental model. Such a model can make them more effective for the rest of their lives.

Another important mental model is a clear picture of what constitutes responsible behavior. To feel good about working in an organization, people must have clear work expectations. They must have a clear mental picture of what they are supposed to do and what others are supposed to do. Often, in the press of daily demands, a manager is too busy to take the time to clarify goals and expectations. Everybody is busy doing something. However, people who are uncer-tain about what is expected of them become frustrated. In such circum-stances, groups often turn against the boss in anger.

Leaders avoid getting bogged down in this swamp of daily activity. They focus their eyes on the horizon and pay attention to things that managers have no time for, such as vision, values, and the organizational climate. By weeding out wasted effort and focusing people on the vision and mission of the organization, they direct their people's energies into positive, purposeful action.

Creating the Conditions Conducive to Self-Esteem

One of the challenges leaders face is creating an organizational climate in which group members' conflicting needs for connectedness, uniqueness, and power can be met simultaneously. Earlier I mentioned that the best organization I have ever worked with is the Kent Fire Department. The people who work there do twice as much with twice as much commitment as any other fire department I know of. I once asked a large group of people in the department what there is about this place that makes it so good. Here are some of their responses:

> "We're a family."
> "I feel respected and appreciated."
> "Camaraderie."
> "I feel safe expressing my feelings or opinions."
> "We don't criticize or condemn each other."
> "It's a two-way street for praise."
> "We love each other."
> "Everybody wants you to succeed here."
> "We take the time to teach new people how this family works."
> "We all believe in the same values."
> "People show their concern for each other."
> "We believe in each other."

All of these statements relate to a sense of connectedness. They emphasize that the members of the department feel a high degree of belonging.

Among other statements were the following:

> "We only hire the best people."
> "I'm in charge of something important."
> "Leaders want to lead because the people are good."

"We claim to be the best and we back it up."

"People want to follow because the leaders are good."

"My opinion is valued and sought out."

"The standards and expectations are high."

"We aren't afraid to make changes."

"I can use my skills here."

"We aren't the average fire department."

"What we do is important."

"We have the opportunity to take risks. It's fun and challenging."

These statements emphasize feelings of autonomy, uniqueness, and power. By meeting these needs and the need for connectedness at the same time, the department has created an organizational climate that fosters the self-esteem of its members. People look forward to coming to work and to excelling in their jobs.

Inviting Participation

One of the most powerful ways of reconciling the conflicting needs for uniqueness, power, and connectedness is to ask for and implement people's ideas for improving things. By asking for their ideas, the leader builds people's feelings of importance and pride in their unique contribution. By implementing their ideas, the leader builds their sense of power or effectiveness because they have had an impact on the organization. At the same time, the leader also builds feelings of worker identification with the organization and hence connectedness. After all, there is now something of each worker in the way the organization does things. Each worker has had a role in making the organization operate the way it does today.

In Japan, companies compete each year for an award given to the company that has received the most worker ideas for improving things. Millions of ideas are received by the companies each year. Seventy-seven percent of Japanese worker suggestions are put into practice, compared to only 26 percent in the United States (Peters, 1989, p. B5). This competition for ideas not only keeps the firms growing but also increases the commitment and self-esteem of the work force.

In North America, workers do not provide as many suggestions. According to Tom Peters (1989, p. B5) the average U.S. worker makes .14 suggestions per year versus 24 per worker per year in Japan. American workers have as many ideas as anyone else, but too often they believe that their suggestions will not be heeded. This belief is often supported by their experience. In such a circumstance, passive "suggestion box" systems will not have much effect. Where no worker suggestions are being heard, the organizational climate diminishes the worker and stifles the growth of the organization.

As a leader, you can change this situation by finding out how many worker suggestions your managers receive and how many of those suggestions they implement. Let managers know that this will be a factor in their performance review. As a result, your managers will seek out suggestions and put as many into practice as possible. The climate will thus change to a collaborative one and the growth and development of the organization will be driven by a new and energetic force.

The effect of this on the enthusiasm of the work force is hard to exaggerate. About six months after Chief Angelo took over the Kent Fire Department, one of his battalion chiefs became alarmed at the volume of work the people were struggling to keep up with. He went to the chief and said, "You've got to ease off. You've given us far too much to do. People are going to burn out. They're going to bust at the seams."

Chief Angelo thought about this a minute and replied, "That's a very alarming statement. Bring me a list of all those extra projects I've given people to do, and we'll see which ones might be put on the back burner for a while."

A few days later the battalion chief was back with a long list of projects that were over and above the normal duties of fire fighters. The chief examined the list. "Where did this first project come from?" he asked.

The battalion chief thought a minute. "I think that was C shift's idea."

"Where did this second project come from?"

"Well, the union wanted that done."

"And what about this third one?"

"Oh, that's fire fighter Smith's pet project."

"And this one?"

"Lieutenant Jones's company thought that up."

They continued through the list and found that every item on it had come from the members of the department. "That's a very interesting list," Chief Angelo concluded. "When you guys get done with it, let me know. Then I'll show you my list."

Had the extra projects been assigned by Chief Angelo, there might have been a great deal of resistance. Because these projects were the fire fighters' own ideas, however, they pursed them with the enthusiasm borne of an opportunity to do something both unique (it was their idea) and powerful (they got to make something happen).

Team Building

In recent years, one of the fads in management training has been team building. Organizations are currently expending much effort on team building, often without giving much thought to why they are doing so. As a consequence, a good deal of the potentially valuable team-building effort is being wasted. In fact, some efforts have left organizations weaker than they were before.

At a team-building retreat, members of a court staff developed some very exciting ideas for improving the court's operation. As the staff members put these ideas forward, however, the court administrator grew more and more defensive. He regarded each idea as a criticism of his management of the organization. Some of the ideas would result in modifications of the changes he had made in the court. At the end of the retreat, the administrator spent an hour rationalizing why each idea could not be put into practice at the present time. The team-building effort thus left the staff discouraged, feeling devalued and powerless to control events. In short, it created the opposite of an esteem-producing climate.

Team-building efforts often fail because no leadership is exercised in the group; there is no vision or understanding of the value of teamwork. Where there is no leadership, there is no commitment, and commitment is essential to teamwork. It is through the act of being led that people become a team.

In becoming part of an effective team, an individual gains a sense of power that is greater than he or she could experience alone. My father, who at the age of sixty took up a new career teaching the bagpipes, is often asked to play solo engagements. In explaining why he also plays in a pipe band with lesser musicians than himself, he says, "The sound of all those instruments playing together is so much greater than anything you could produce yourself, and yet you have the sense that you are playing it." This is the feeling that people have when they work together in effective teams.

Teams and the Authority to Think. Managers sometimes refer to their people as a team when in reality they are merely a collection of individuals. As explained in Chapter Six, teams are distinguished by the fact that all members participate in the thinking, in deciding how the group will go about achieving its results. If a manager retains the authority to think, assigning individual tasks to his or her people, there will be no sense of teamwork, and no amount of calling people a team will give them that sense. To function as a team, people must be involved in deciding what the team will do. By participating in decision making, individuals gain a sense of uniqueness and power while also gaining a sense of connectedness to a group. Thus, two potentially conflicting needs are met simultaneously. This unleashes tremendous motivation and a feeling of satisfaction in the individual team members.

When Teams Are Appropriate. Teams are most effective in situations where an individual cannot own a whole product. For example, in a hospital operating room, one person cannot do everything necessary to achieve the result of correcting whatever is wrong with the patient. This requires many pairs of hands working in coordination. Similarly, in some situations more technical skills than any one person could possess must be brought together to fulfill a desired result.

When I talked about giving people ownership, I used the example of eliminating fragmentation by allowing people to do the many tasks necessary to delivering a service rather than requiring them to do one thing repetitively. In some cases, the tasks are of such a technical nature that it would take one person a lifetime to develop all the requisite skills. In the case of environmentally sensitive forestry work, for example, it is better to have a team of a forester and a fish biologist look at the best way to harvest logs without damaging streams than to expect a fish biologist to have the equivalent of a degree in silviculture.

It is important to note that there are times when teamwork is not desirable or appropriate. One highly effective internal consulting group in a large government agency, for example, changed its approach and had people work in teams instead of as individuals on its projects. The subsequent division of the work effort made things take longer and also diluted the sense of accomplishment each worker got from doing the job. By contrast, when a highway department installed computer-aided design and drafting software, it eliminated the position of draftsperson and allowed the designers to do two jobs simultaneously. The job satisfaction and enthusiasm of the designers rose because they now had more control over the final product.

Avoiding Criticism and Fostering an Invitational Climate

One of the greatest enemies of a positive work climate is the natural tendency of most people to criticize each other. This is a natural tendency because of the way people are motivated. Our self-image is composed of a multisensory "picture" of who we are at present and a world-view, or a multisensory image of what the world around us is like. Moment to moment, our brain is involved in comparing our images of ourselves and the world with incoming sensory information. When we notice disparities, we take action to try to close the gap either by changing our behavior or by trying to change the situation (Glasser, 1984, pp. 159–170).

Imagine two co-workers, Julie and Charlie. If Julie behaves in ways that do not meet the part of Charlie's world-view that contains his expectations of co-worker behavior, Charlie will tend to take direct action. Unfortunately, it seems to Charlie that the way to do this is to tell Julie what is wrong with her behavior, to tell her how much better off she would be if she behaved in a different manner. He may engage her in conversation to tell her what her "problem is" or to give her five reasons why she is wrong to behave the way she does. Such criticism rarely has a positive outcome, however. The reason for this is that Julie also has a world-view, and in that world-view, there is something wrong with people who tell her what her problems are. She therefore does not look at Charlie's statement as evidence that she has a problem but that he has one. He shouldn't behave that way.

Julie also has a sense of her present self, one that comes under attack when she is told that her behavior is somehow deficient. Since the image is a whole-brain picture, billions of neurons simultaneously detect a disparity, providing her with a quick jolt of confusion, a quick sense that something is very wrong. To cope with this, she quickly rejects the incoming information. Her instinctive reaction is to say to herself, "No! That's not right." When she rejects the statement as untrue, the disparity between her world-view and what she perceives is eliminated.

Charlie's approach is therefore bound to fail. It is also likely to create in Julie's mind the idea that Charlie has a problem because his behavior does not match her view of how a co-worker should act. Distrust and animosity between the two are likely to result, making it difficult for all other members of the group to feel that they are part of an effective team. Because each group member believes it would be better if the others behaved according to his or her own world view, the possibilities of conflict are high. Creating a noncritical environment is thus one of the main tasks of a leader.

Many leadership acts discussed previously contribute to the building of a noncritical, invitational climate. One way in which leaders do this is by inviting all members to become involved in the creation of a vision of what the organization will be like in the future and in the determination of group values and norms, as described earlier. By involving people in this process, leaders allow each one to participate in the creation of a common world-view, at least as far as work is concerned. If the world-view portion of people's self-images match, then there will be less chance of conflict.

Leaders also contribute to a noncritical, invitational climate by delegating the right to fail. As already pointed out, leaders expect occasional failures because they have high performance expectations of their people. They delegate the right to fail as long as people learn from the experience. In this way, the failure makes the organization stronger, not weaker.

Validations also contribute to a noncritical climate. When people are criticized, they are told negative things about their personal qualities. They are branded (often in their own minds, at least) as incapable, irresponsible, stupid, or lazy. We have seen the esteem-robbing and conflict-producing consequences of such a situation. Validating an individual's positive qualities is the opposite of criticizing the person, and it tends to have the opposite effects. If people become used to hearing validations from the leader, they may become more comfortable giving them to each other. Validation enhances connectedness because it creates a bond between the validator and the individual whose personal quality is being validated. It simultaneously enhances a sense of uniqueness.

Encouraging Self-Confidence and Risk Taking

When the organizational climate is positive and people have high self-esteem, they are able to risk. That is, they are willing to do something new, different, not comfortable. It means people are willing to move beyond the familiar to the potentially better.

As I have said all along, no leadership is being exercised in an organization that is standing still, that is still doing today what it did yesterday. The ability to risk is thus essential to leadership. If the leader does not create a climate in which people feel willing to risk, her efforts to lead will meet with resistance. People will cling to the safety of the old ways of doing things. As with the other areas we have discussed in this chapter, what is good for the follower is also good for the leader and for the organization.

Taking a risk requires self-confidence. Leaders encourage people to follow them when their interactions with the leader boost the people's self-confidence. Leaders breed self-confidence by establishing a climate of growth—that is, they not only create effective systems, they also prepare their people to succeed in those systems by holding people responsible for learning rather than for perfect performance. Leaders are more concerned that people develop self-confidence than that they are confident in the leader. One reason for this concern is that self-confident people do better work and hence create a more effective organization. In turn, people in effective organizations tend to feel more confidence in themselves. Another reason is that people are more willing to follow those who have confidence in them. Paradoxically, however, one has difficulty perceiving the leader's confidence if one lacks confidence in oneself.

Taking risks also requires strong feelings of connectedness. People who feel that they are not fully accepted by other members of the group are often timid about taking a risky position. They feel that to do so would jeopardize their standing in the group. If they feel trusted and accepted, however, they are more able to risk.

Aversion to risk is also reduced if people have clear goals. As Clemes and Bean (1981, p. 244) point out, "new experiences are chosen only if they make sense in terms of some goal." By focusing people on the outcome instead of the process, leaders create a climate more hospitable to risk.

Building Equality in the Sense of Who We Are

Where there are distinctions between classes of people in the workplace, the sense of connectedness is reduced or destroyed and performance is likely to dwindle. Too often, for instance, clerical people are treated as second-class citizens of an organization. This is true even in human service organizations, where leaders pride themselves on being people oriented. Clerical people are often excluded from meetings of "professional staff," thereby kept in the dark about what is happening. They are rarely given uninterrupted time in which to finish important projects or offered opportunities for their own professional development. This makes clerical work "just a job" for these people. They are not committed to doing their best for the organization because the organization doesn't do its best for them.

Volunteers are even more likely to be treated this way. As with clerical people, volunteers are often not invited to staff meetings, are kept in the dark about policy shifts, and are rarely given training. In addition, volunteers often have no work space. Staff members sometimes forget that volunteers are coming in and have nothing planned for them. The resulting sense of exclusion inhibits total commitment. It leads to turnover, which in turn leads to staff criticism of volunteers for being unreliable. On the contrary, volunteers are very reliable. If they are not given a sense of being equal and important members of the team, they can be relied upon to quit.

Even individuals sensitive to this issue sometimes inadvertently create a gulf between volunteers and paid staff. They forget that much of what goes on in an agency is an ever-evolving process. Paid staff know today what has happened in the past few days, but volunteer staff usually do not. Because volunteers are not at the agency every day, salaried employees need to make a special effort to bring them up-to-date on what has been going on in their absence.

Leaders contribute to the sense of equality and connectedness by sharing information about the organizations's plans, problems, and financial situation freely with their people. Where people are informed only on a "need to know" basis, they often feel confused about the organization's direction. Secrets make those not privy to them feel excluded, not connected.

Secrets also make it hard for people to develop good ideas for improving the way the organization works. Managers frequently lament the "half-baked" or ill-thought-out nature of people's suggestions. When people are kept in the dark, however, their suggestions will seldom be enlightened. Because of this, everybody needs to know as much as possible.

Sometimes members' sense of equality in an organization is weakened because one person's abilities are superior to others'. The star performer may get all the praise and attention. Leaders can prevent this by talking of the star performer's success as evidence of the way "we" do things. Others' efforts therefore are bolstered, not diminished, by the legendary feats of the few.

Feelings of equality can also be diminished when one member of a team fails in his or her responsibilities and the team does not achieve its desired results. In dysfunctional groups, people tend to blame someone else for all their misfortunes, never accepting responsibility themselves. This leads to an endless round of blaming and criticism. It focuses people on what they cannot control—their past behavior—making them feel powerless and depressed. Leaders combat this by turning their people's attention away from the setback and toward the future. Leaders get people to look at what they will do differently next time. To keep members from focusing on the person who has failed, leaders ask each member, "How will *you* do better in the future?" This directs people's attention to what they can control—their own future behavior—and produces a healthier, more optimistic climate.

Feelings of equality give people a sense of connectedness and contribute to the sense of "who we are." Leaders facilitate this by helping their people enunciate a common purpose and common values. If the climate is to be a positive one, the common purpose must, of course, be stated in positive terms. Mission and vision statements should therefore express what the organization is trying to accomplish, not what it is trying to prevent. Beliefs such as "We provide superior service," for instance, create a mental model that inspires people to feel confident. As Senge (1984, p. 225) points out, "negative visions carry a subtle yet unmistakable message of powerlessness." Thus, for example, the purpose of ensuring a loving home for every child is more powerful than one of preventing child abuse.

Organizations also communicate their attitude toward their people through the quality of their equipment and physical surroundings. Leaders can help make people feel special by making sure that these things are as good as the organization's budget will allow. As the leader of one nonprofit agency remarks, "If something breaks, get it off the floor, get it fixed, get it back. While it's broken, it shouldn't just sit there. If the paint gets chipped, you scrape it down and paint it. We keep up with things. It's an attitude I have" (National Assembly of National Voluntary Health and Social Welfare Organizations, 1989, p. 66).

Of course, nonprofit organizations are usually strapped for resources. Managers often use this fact to justify a lack of equipment. And indeed, if they were to spend money that could be used for client services on fancy furniture, staff members might view that as contrary to the organization's values. Nevertheless, managers must be careful about not sending their people a message that they are second-class citizens in a second-class organization. One city department head asked his staff what additional office furnishings they wanted. One of their requests was for oak cabinets. The staff did not really expect to get them. Indeed, even used oak cabinets proved beyond the budgetary limits of the department. But when the leader purchased cabinets with oak trim, it sent people a message that he was trying his best to meet their needs. That quarter-inch piece of oak became a symbol that he cared about them. It meant that they mattered.

Where there is positive leadership, a positive sense of who we are pervades the organization. It is communicated in the organizational self-talk, what people say to each other about the organization. By creating a positive organizational climate, leaders help the individual members feel good about their involvement in the organization. Such a climate makes legendary performance possible.

EPILOGUE

A revolution is currently under way in the private sector. It is a revolution that places maximum value on the frontline employee and on responsiveness to the customer. Organizations not signing on with that revolution are floundering in their own bureaucratic waste. In the nonprofit and, especially, the public sectors, people have been slower to join the revolution. In part, the reason is that government organizations find it difficult to move quickly because civil service rules, administrative codes, and even laws must sometimes be changed to bring about a better situation. Nonetheless, leaders at all levels in these organizations are turning their followers away from business as usual to find more effective ways of serving people.

Freeing organizations from the complacency of past procedures is a task for the nineties. It is the task of the new leader in the nonprofit and governmental worlds. It is the task of the person who seeks to focus the full potential of his or her people on creating better communities. Effective leadership brings about performance that is memorable and worthy of praise. Such leadership encourages legendary performance.

In this book, we have looked at leaders from three perspectives. First, we have looked at the kinds of qualities effective leaders possess and how they influence others to follow. Second, we have examined the systems leaders create to bring out the best in their people. Finally we have considered the relationship of leaders to the people they lead.

Leaders Themselves

People can do a number of things to enhance their personal and status-based power. Simply stated, however, to lead effectively, people must think differently than ordinary people do.

Leaders are first of all proactive people. The essence of leadership in the government and nonprofit sectors is bringing people together to make change that results in better service. To do this, leaders must have a different way of thinking about impediments to success. They must avoid an "I can't do that because" mind-set. In government and nonprofit organizations, managers tend to use laws, regulations, policies, and the standards of their accrediting bodies as excuses for inaction. Where managers say, "That's a good idea, but it's against the rules," leadership is lacking. Leaders make change, encourage new legislation, lobby for different policies, change systems, and sometimes even break bureaucratic rules to create better results for the organization. Leaders are in the habit of asking, "How can we do that?"

Ordinary managers often ask, "How are things going?" and are relieved to hear that they are going well. Leaders ask, "How can we improve this?" even when things are going well. They also ask their people, "What have you changed lately?" and "What new ideas have you considered?" to establish an expectation of constant improvement.

Leaders are people with a single-minded devotion to the purpose of the group they are leading. This commitment, I believe, stems from the way leaders occupy their minds. A person's level of commitment to a purpose is commensurate with the amount of time she or he devotes to thinking about it. Committed people devote the majority of their thoughts to the people the agency is trying to serve.

They spend their time thinking about the needs of those people and what their organizations can do to meet those needs. Such a focus produces passionate devotion to the purpose of the organization. Less effective people, on the other hand, allow their thoughts to be consumed by the mundane aspects of their personal lives, political intrigue, or the process of getting things done. As a result, their attention is sidetracked from the purpose of their work. Effective leaders manage to dwell instead on the outcome they are trying to achieve. A single-minded devotion to the organization's purpose is the hallmark of the effective leader.

Leaders and Systems

The changes that leaders make do not stem from their own unique vision. Effective leaders articulate the needs and dreams of their followers. They give shape to the unformed desires of their people and give them hope of achieving them. By doing this, leaders align the efforts of their people behind an important mission.

Leaders also think in terms of whole systems. They are able to see how the system of doing the work affects the motivation and commitment of their people. Simply stated, leaders get the demotivating and inefficient aspects of the work system out of people's way. Leaders encourage legendary performance by creating systems that enable people to find fulfillment, satisfaction, and enjoyment in their daily work lives.

In service organizations, the essence of creating an effective system is to match positions to customers. Unfortunately, most service organizations are not organized this way. Jobs are matched to processes, and customers (clients or citizens) get the runaround in such a fragmented system. By redefining job responsibilities so that people are responsible for the customer, leaders ensure fast and effective service and a rewarding work life for their people.

Although leaders are constantly engaged in improving systems, they avoid getting bogged down in processes and always insist on results. For example, Dana Badgerow, director of the Minnesota Department of General Administration, followed up a recommendation of a group of support personnel with a demand that her division heads report progress to her on implementing the recommendations. Leaders insist on getting action from their people.

Leaders and Their People

The most fundamental aspect of the relationship between effective leaders and their people is the degree of empowerment of the workers. Leaders create situations in which people feel in control of their work lives. Leaders do this in part by creating efficient systems so that volunteers and staff can work effectively to make things happen, but they also do it in their daily interactions with people. Effective leaders enhance their people's sense of control, in part, by giving them the authority to make decisions and act quickly within the framework of clear organizational values. They have faith in their people and in the future their people can create. They keep their people from dwelling on the past, which cannot be controlled, and direct them toward what they can do in the future.

This focus on the future leads to proactive effort. Most people in our society work reactively. They work on something because they fear not meeting a deadline rather than because they think it is a good idea. Their lives at work are controlled by others. By encouraging proactive rather than reactive effort, leaders help people feel more optimistic and hopeful.

By following the practical advice contained in this book, managers can create a situation in which committed, self-confident people work in exciting jobs that build their self-esteem. They can create an organization with coordinated energy focused on the achievement of a worthwhile mission.

REFERENCES

Albrecht, K. *Service Within: Solving the Middle Management Leadership Crisis.* Homewood, Ill.: Dow Jones-Irwin, 1990.

Carver, J. *Boards That Make a Difference: A New Design for Leadership in Nonprofit and Public Organizations.* San Francisco: Jossey-Bass, 1990.

Clemes, H., and Bean, R. *Self-Esteem.* New York: Putnam, 1981.

Covey, S. R. *The Seven Habits of Highly Effective People: Restoring the Character Ethic.* New York: Fireside, 1990.

"The Cracks in Quality." *Economist,* 1992, *323*(7755), 67–68.

Crosby, P. *Quality Without Tears.* New York: McGraw-Hill, 1984.

Drucker, P. "Management and the World's Work." *Harvard Business Review,* 1988, *66*(5), 65–76.

Drucker, P. "The New Productivity Challenge." *Harvard Business Review,* 1991, *69*(6), 69–79.

Glasser, W. *Control Theory.* New York: Harper & Row, 1984.

Grove, A. S. *High Output Management.* New York: Vintage Books, 1985.

Hall, J., and Donnell, S. M. "Bureaupathic Management: The Quiet Crisis in Government." In Jay Hall, *Models for Management: The Structure of Competence.* Woodlands, Tex.: Woodstead Press, 1988.

Hanrahan, T. F. "New Approaches to Caregiving." *Healthcare Forum Journal*, July/Aug. 1991, pp. 33–37.

Hersey, P. *The Situational Leader*. New York: Warner Books, 1984.

Ilsley, P. J., *Enhancing the Volunteer Experience*. San Francisco: Jossey-Bass, 1990.

Johnson, P. T. "Why I Race Against Phantom Competitors." *Harvard Business Review*, 1988, *66*(5), 106–112.

Kennedy, L. W. *Quality Management in the Nonprofit World*. San Francisco: Jossey-Bass, 1991.

Kouzes, J. M., and Posner, B. Z. *The Leadership Challenge: How to Get Extraordinary Things Done in Organizations*. San Francisco: Jossey-Bass, 1989.

Loehr, J. E., and McLaughlin, P. J., *Mentally Tough*. Toronto: Totem Books, 1987.

Lynch, R. *Precision Management: How to Build and Lead the Winning Organization*. Seattle: Abbott Press, 1988.

Lynch, R. *Getting Out of Your Own Way*. Seattle: Abbott Press, 1989.

Lynch, R., and McCurley, S. *Essential Volunteer Management*. Downers Grove, Ill.: Heritage Arts, 1989.

MacKenzie, R. A. *The Time Trap*. New York: McGraw-Hill, 1975.

National Assembly of National Voluntary Health and Social Welfare Organizations. *A Study in Excellence: Management in the Nonprofit Human Services*. Washington, D.C.: National Assembly of National Voluntary Health and Social Welfare Organizations, 1989.

Osborne, D. "Ten Ways to Turn D.C. Around." *Washington Post Magazine*, Dec. 9, 1990.

O'Toole, P. "Life in the Electronic Office." *Lears*, 1991, *4*(5), 21–22.

Peters, T. "The Name of the Game Is Constant Improvement." *Seattle Post-Intelligencer*, Oct. 4, 1988, p. B6.

Peters, T. "Melodrama? U.S. Business Situation Is No Exaggeration." *Seattle Post-Intelligencer*, Feb. 14, 1989, p. B5.

Peters, T. J., and Waterman, R. H. *In Search of Excellence: Lessons from America's Best Run Companies*. New York: Harper & Row, 1982.

"Reinventing Companies." *Economist*, 1991, *321*(7727), 67.

Robbins, A. *Awaken the Giant Within*. New York: Summit Books, 1991.

Schaffer, R. H., and Thomson, H. A. "Successful Change Programs Begin with Results." *Harvard Business Review*, 1992, *70*(1), 80-91.

Schlesinger, L., and Heskett, J. "The Service Driven Service Company." *Harvard Business Review*, 1991, *69*(5), 71-81.

Seligman, M.E.P. *Learned Optimism*. New York: Knopf, 1991.

Senge, P. M. *The Fifth Discipline*. New York: Doubleday, 1990.

Sensenbrenner, J. "Quality Comes to City Hall." *Harvard Business Review*, 1991, *69*(2), 64-75.

Siler, J. F., and Garland, S. "Sending Health Care into Rehab." *Business Week*, Oct. 25, 1991, pp. 111-112.

Teal, T. "Service Comes First: An Inteview with Robert F. McDermott." *Harvard Business Review*, 1991, *69*(5), 116-127.

"Washington's Mayor: Less Bang for the Same Buck." *Economist*, 1991, *321*(7738), 30.

Weber, D. O., "Six Models of Patient-Focused Care." *Healthcare Forum Journal*, July/Aug. 1991, pp. 23-31.

Williams, A. L. *All You Can Do Is All You Can Do, But All You Can Do Is Enough*. New York: Ballantine, 1988.

Zaleznik, A. *The Managerial Mystique: Restoring Leadership in Business*. New York: Harper & Row, 1989.

Zaleznik, A. "The Human Dilemmas of Leadership." In Harvard Business Review, *People: Managing Your Most Important Asset*. Boston: Harvard Business Review, 1990.

Zaleznik, A. "Retrospective Commentary." *Harvard Business Review*, 1992, *70*(2), 130-131.

INDEX